the magenta principles™

Engagement, depth and challenge in the classroom

by Mike Hughes

Published by:
Magenta Principles Limited
4 Vineyards Close
Cheltenham
GL53 8NH

ISBN 978-0-9930788-0-4

Editor: Alan Everett
Design and layout: Chris Kear

Printed in the UK by:
Gomer Press
Llandysul
Ceredigion
Wales

Contents

Thanks to…

A huge number of people have contributed in a great many different ways to this publication and I would like to thank each and every one of them. It would be impossible to mention everyone by name on this page but I would like to take this opportunity to acknowledge the contribution of the following people:

- A massive thank you to all of the teachers who have sent me examples of how they have used the Magenta Principles in the classroom. A comprehensive list of individual teachers who have contributed to this book can be found on page 217 and the names of the schools involved are listed on page 5. It is a huge shame that a lack of space prevented me from including every contribution I received.

- The staff at Whitley Bay High School deserve a special mention for their contribution and cooperation. Particular thanks to Adam Chedburn for agreeing to write the Foreword and to Rachel Mays, Linda Buckle and Alan Keegan for their contribution to the case study.

- Gemma Gilbert, Emma Johns, Joanna Rousseau, Tom Walton, Nigel Cross, Chris Holmwood and Rachel Hayward have all made a particularly significant contribution and I am enormously grateful for their help and support.

- Chris Kear and Alan Everett for turning a manuscript into a book.

- Many thanks to all those people and organisations that have given permission to reproduce extracts of their work. Further details can be found on page 218.

- Everyone and everything that helped to keep my spirits up and made me smile when the frustrations of writing began to mount. Although they will never know, Bruce Springsteen, Elmer, Jaffa Cakes and Joel Monaghan have all played a role in this publication.

- Rach, Ben and Sam – apologies and thanks in equal measure.

Schools

The following schools have contributed to this publication. They are listed in the order in which they appear in the book.

- Whitley Bay High School
- Sidmouth CE Primary School
- Wymondham High Academy
- Lutterworth College
- The Ecclesbourne School
- Ysgol Bro Dinefwr, Llandeilo
- Trinity School, Carlisle
- Yenton Primary School, Erdington, Birmingham
- St Augustine's RC High School, Billington, Lancashire
- Pinders Primary School, Wakefield
- Richard Bonington Primary and Nursery School, Nottingham
- Carlton le Willows Academy, Nottingham
- Chiltern Training Group
- All Saints Catholic School, Dagenham
- Brinsworth Comprehensive School, Rotherham
- The Brunts Academy, Mansfield
- Ian Ramsey School, Stockton-on-Tees
- Ysgol Gyfun Gymraeg Bro Myrddin, Croesyceiliog
- Shenley Brook End School, Milton Keynes
- St Thomas More Catholic School, Blaydon-upon-Tyne
- Bonnygate Primary School, South Ockendon

We really wanted to improve when we met Mike and the Magenta Principles became the explicit vehicle that set us on our way.

Foreword

by Adam Chedburn

There are those who think that great learning occurs through lots of eureka moments, and then there are those who believe it to be more gradual, more multi-paced – and Mike Hughes would have it as *messy*. I don't believe that the moment when Mike stood in our school hall and first introduced us to the Magenta Principles™ was a eureka moment, or maybe it was, but we didn't recognise it as such at the time. It was more like one of those moments when a pebble skims the surface of a pond and sets off a whole sequence of ripples. For some slow learners like myself, it took a while to even remember what the Magenta Principles were – Mike had often referred to red and blue (see page 180); we'd got that, but magenta? Over the last 12 years, however, they have become deeply embedded in our teaching approach and this book exemplifies how schools that really want to make learning and teaching improve can work with ideas, customise, adapt and personalise them, and affect the learning experience of students. Mike often says, *if you want something to happen, make it explicit, don't leave it to chance.* We really wanted to improve when we first met him, and the Magenta Principles became the explicit vehicle that set us on our way.

We have been working with Mike Hughes for most of this century, and the impact of his ideas has been profound. However, the impact has become embedded because we've been brave, we've talked at length about his key messages, we've adapted and customised them, and most importantly we've grown as teachers through the dialogue and the sheer fun we've had experimenting, refining and improving. We have lived our professional development through 'tweaking to transform'. Early on, Mike asked where our next 5% would come from – we came to the conclusion that it could only come from our passion to excite and enthral.

Cont...

In 2013 Ofsted judged Whitley Bay High School to be outstanding.

They also described teaching as exciting and innovative.

I believe in the felicific calculus – how happy your staff are equates to how happy your students are. This may sound trite, but happy, engaged staff who get it will have a powerful impact on making students the same. Great teachers don't need or crave the bauble of Ofsted judgements, they crave the adrenalin rush when they leave a lesson knowing that they have facilitated great learning. As Mike says – *if Ofsted described one of my lessons as outstanding but I knew the kids had been bored, I would personally not judge it to be a success.*

Headteachers must constantly ask themselves: is there anything I'm doing that hinders staff from being the best teachers they can be? If we say teaching and learning is our core purpose, does the way we run meetings and training in our school truly reflect this in our practice? And lastly we must ask: what do we hope to achieve by grading lessons? Do children gain more confidence by being constantly labelled? Do teachers?

There is a passage in *Alice in Wonderland* in which Alice meets the Cheshire Cat at a crossroads and asks which way she should go. *That* replies the Cat *depends on where you want to get to.* Alice answers that she doesn't much mind, to which the Cat responds: *Then it doesn't matter which way you go.* I am sure every Headteacher in the country knows which way they want to go; they want to have strikingly exciting lessons that engage students, promote enquiry and reflection, and combine rigour with fun. The dilemma is, does this translate into an outstanding grade from Ofsted?

This book is about the Magenta Principles and how they have been a powerful influence over time to improve our learning and teaching. In 2013, Ofsted not only judged our school to be outstanding, but also described our lessons as *exciting and innovative*, adding *there is a buzz amongst adults and students in the classroom.* This surely is the ultimate proof that you can have both.

Adam Chedburn
Headteacher
Whitley Bay High School 1993 – 2014

The Magenta Principles™ is simply an umbrella term referring to the way in which students can interact with information, and was adopted to provide a common language and shared vocabulary that many schools and teachers find useful.

Think engagement, challenge and depth and you're on the right lines.

Introduction

The Magenta Principles™ were conceived in Halesowen. To be precise, the germ of an idea first popped into my head as I was walking down the English corridor having just covered a lesson for an absent colleague. Although I didn't know it at the time, the Magenta Principles were born, and although they have been added to, refined and amended a great many times since, their origin can be traced back to that cover lesson all those years ago. Many people speculate where the phrase comes from – that is my secret and will remain so!

In a nutshell, the Magenta Principles is an umbrella phrase that refers to a philosophy and an approach to teaching based upon the premise that learning should be both exciting and engaging. More specifically, the phrase represents a pedagogy underpinned by an unshakeable belief that:

- learning is the consequence of thinking… therefore our job is to get them to think
- language is central to thinking… therefore our job is to get them to talk
- learning is an active process… therefore our job is to get them doing.

We talk about the Magenta Principles – but in reality there is just one principle; in order to make sense of the information that comes their way, children have to do something to/with it. Receiving it, retaining it and eventually regurgitating it is insufficient – in short, they have to think about it! The receive, retain and regurgitate approach may get a child through an examination hoop but it will not develop a deep understanding, and while all teachers want to help children pass exams some of us want much more – we want them to get it, get why they got it and, as much as anything, enjoy it.

The question therefore becomes: **What are children required to do to with the information they encounter in the classroom?** It is central to the approach and the answer gives us the Magenta Principles – children could be asked to reduce it, change it, assemble it, add to it, arrange it, sequence it, classify it…the list goes on and on.

The Magenta Principles – and therefore this book – are most certainly not a catalogue of lesson plans or collection of good ideas. Rather they have a nebulous, intangible dimension that resists capture in written form. Think more abstract than concrete; more principles to adapt than strategies to adopt; more spirit, ethos, philosophy than resource, activity or game. Not surprisingly, it has been a hard book to write for the recipe is not the flavour.

While all teachers want to help students pass exams, some of us want much more – we want them to get it, get why they got it and, as much as anything, enjoy it.

To stay with the recipe metaphor a little longer, it is also worth stating from the outset that the Magenta Principles are not ready meals – it is a phrase that is used throughout the book. In much the same way that the quality of the culinary experience is dependent more on the chef than the list of ingredients, so the quality and depth of the learning is dependent more on the facilitation than the resources (this idea is explored in more depth on pages 147-155).

Some of the core ideas were first published as far back as 1997 in *Lessons are for Learning* – although at that time I was only using the term Magenta Principles in private. The phrase Magenta Principles was used publicly for the first time in 2006 in *And the Main Thing is… Learning*. Since then, literally thousands of teachers have attended my Magenta Principles workshops and the phrase is now heard on a daily basis in a great many schools. In response to an abundance of requests, I have finally decided to pull all of the Magenta Principles ideas together in one publication.

Books capture a moment in time, and it is worth bearing in mind that words may be in vogue at the time of writing but out of fashion by the time they are read. It is important to make explicit that these words have not been written because they are the prevailing orthodoxy or as a response to the latest initiative; they have been written because they reflect the way in which people learn and are based upon a belief that pedagogy should be driven by learning. For while governments change, the economy fluctuates and initiatives wax and wane, children remain children and learning remains learning, and our job is, was and always will be to help children learn.

Mike Hughes
Cheltenham 2014

A book with a difference

This is a book with a difference; not so much a book for you to read but more a book for you to write.

If our goal was to make learning an engaging, student-centred experience then the Magenta Principles was the vehicle that enabled us to get there.

Whitley Bay High School

A book to write

The Magenta Principles are not a collection of activities or an approach to be adopted, but more a set of principles to be adapted. For off-the-peg solutions rarely work. They may be quicker and generally more convenient, but the fit is always better when tailored to the individual context.

Whitley Bay High School (WBHS) in the North East is the school that has taken the Magenta Principles to heart more than any other (their story is told in more detail on pages 201-213). In their own words:

> "if our goal was to make learning an engaging, student-centred experience then the Magenta Principles was the vehicle that enabled us to get there."

There are some key words in that statement: *our, vehicle, us.* For WBHS did not simply adopt the Magenta Principles, they adapted them. More than that they developed and customised them and, over a number of years, arrived at a pedagogy that is theirs. They did it – the Magenta Principles were just a vehicle; a vehicle that helped them go on a most amazing journey.

The process of internalising – or Whitley Baying as they call it – is crucial. Staff at the school understand and commit to the approach, not least because they have been fully involved in developing it. Consequently, teachers are not using Magenta Principles activities because they are expected to or for the sake of it, but because of a deeply held belief that they promote exciting and effective learning.

WBHS is by no means alone in using the Magenta Principles as a vehicle to enhance classroom practice. Schools such as Sidmouth CE Primary School, Wymondham High Academy and Lutterworth College have their own tales to tell of how they have taken the basic ideas expressed in this book and applied them in their own unique context. They too are on a journey – their journey. There may have been different starting points, they may be taking slightly different routes, but they are heading for the same destination – lessons that engage and excite.

The purpose behind this book is not for you to read about their journeys, but to inspire you to embark on your own. Resist the temptation to adopt, implement and replicate; your challenge is to adapt, interpret and develop. In other words, write your own book.

Before you pick up your pen, it might help to have an understanding of how the Magenta Principles came to be.

Most teachers think subject/context and strategies, i.e. *I teach maths or art or Year 4. That's a useful strategy for teaching Year 8 maths, but I teach art so it's no use to me.*

It is a mindset that makes disseminating good ideas difficult.

The beginning

Let us begin at the beginning. Four lessons are central to the Magenta Principle's story; four lessons and the kaleidoscope of ideas, connections and questions they provoked. The fact that both the lessons and the thinking that surrounded them are recounted here in linear, bullet-point format is a little misleading and disguises the enormous complexity of a thought process that included as many cul-de-sacs and blind alleys as it did moments of clarity and insight. Nonetheless, the Magenta Principles, like all things, are at their most effective when they are understood, and to understand the Magenta Principles it is important to have an appreciation of how they came to be.

Lesson one

Many years ago I had the pleasure of observing what, to this day, I regard as one of the best maths lessons I have ever seen.

Using an overhead projector the teacher presented the class with twenty sums (mathematicians would probably call them problems or calculations, but to me they were sums) with the single instruction to do the three hardest. As the lesson progressed the teacher began to probe a little deeper: *I notice you've all gone for number 19; what makes 19 harder than the rest? Did you have to do 19 differently then? How could we make the others as hard as 19? Jenny, I notice that you've gone for 11 but Chris has gone for number 7 – you've got 30 seconds to convince him that 11 is harder than 7.* And so on.

It was brilliant; simple but hugely effective. Three things struck me as I watched the lesson unfold:

- How such a simple strategy could lead to such effective learning
- How the task had been the catalyst for an enormous amount of constructive dialogue
- How the teacher had helped the students articulate and therefore clarify and deepen their thinking through very skilful questioning.

However, when I enthusiastically described the lesson to the rest of the staff at our daily briefing, a rather cynical voice grunted from the back: *I don't teach maths.* A couple of sniggers broke the otherwise awkward silence and it was apparent that not everyone shared my enthusiasm! My balloon was well and truly pricked and as I sulked in my office I reflected on how difficult it is to disseminate good ideas when the prevailing mindset is firmly based upon subject and strategy.

We need to think less about subject/context-specific **strategies** and more about generic **principles.**

These principles can then be **applied** to any particular context.

Lesson two

A few days later I covered the English lesson referred to in the introduction, only to be informed that no work had been set but that the group had just finished reading *Romeo and Juliet*. This was little help to me as, at the time, I knew next to nothing about the play. Instinct kicked in and I enquired who the key character was; rather predictably the instant response from the boy on my left was Romeo while the girl on my right insisted that it was actually Juliet.

I duly remarked what a good title it was and, as I was frantically thinking how I might spin this out for an hour, a voice from the back suggested that *there wouldn't have been much of story if Friar Lawrence hadn't married them.* This was quickly followed up with the comment that *the nurse had a lot to answer for,* while a number of students insisted that Tybalt did more than his fair share of stirring. I spent the next twenty minutes posing questions, asking for justification, playing devil's advocate and generally chairing a debate with the only rule being that opinions had to be backed up with evidence, reasons and/or examples. It was one of my better cover lessons, even if I do say so myself!

Three things struck me as I walked down the English corridor:

- The difference between instruction and facilitation. I had taught a perfectly good lesson without knowing anything about the content. Indeed, it seems the more a teacher knows about a subject the more they are inclined to talk.
- Good teachers need things 'up their sleeve'.
- Most significantly, however, I made the crucial connection between the English lesson that I had just taught and the maths lesson that I had witnessed just a few days earlier…and what we now refer to as the Magenta Principles were born. On both occasions, children had been asked to *reduce* information.

It was the third point that was particularly significant and I began to tentatively hypothesise that:

- We need to think less about teaching maths or English and more about teaching children. More specifically, we need to think of our job as being to help children learn.
- We need to think less about subject/context-specific strategies and more about generic principles. These principles can then be applied to any particular context.

…the exercise sparked off all sorts of interesting dialogue, presented numerous opportunities for me to extend their thinking through careful questioning and gave me a real insight into the way in which individuals were thinking.

Pick out the key words in the comment above

- Sparked
- Opportunities
- Dialogue
- Extend
- Insight

Anyone can present students with a piece of text and ask them to highlight the key words. The key, however, is the reference to the teacher extending their thinking through careful questioning.

If two teachers employed the same Magenta Principle activity with parallel groups in adjacent classrooms, it is a fair bet that there would be different levels of learning taking place in the two rooms.

The task is the constant, the variable the teacher, and there are implications here for professional development.

Lesson three

The next challenge was to apply my experiences in maths and English to my own curriculum area of geography. What emerged was a lesson that was first described in *Lessons are for Learning* as far back as 1997 (see page 219 for more details).

The plan was simple; present the students with a paragraph that outlined the process of onion-skin weathering and ask them to highlight what they considered to be the six key words. They worked individually, then in a small group and finally as a whole class to whittle down the dozen or so words that had originally been identified as significant to the required six. Simple, but again highly effective in that the exercise sparked off all sorts of interesting dialogue, presented numerous opportunities for me to extend their thinking through careful questioning and gave me a real insight into the way in which individuals were thinking.

Simon – a young colleague – had observed the lesson and was impressed with what he had seen. Interestingly, however, he struggled to articulate precisely why the lesson had been so impressive and found it difficult to identify how the experience could improve his own teaching. It was only when it was made explicit that the lesson had been based upon the principle of *reducing information* that the penny dropped and he could begin to identify ways in which he could apply the same principle to his particular subject area. We now had a shared vocabulary and we were on our way.

Dilemma

At this point it may be worthwhile reading the section entitled *Principles not strategies*, as the fourth lesson – which is described overleaf – takes us off on something of a tangent. However, it is a crucial strand of the narrative and demands inclusion: the dilemma being, at what point to include it.

That decision is left to you!

- Option A is to skip ahead and read *Principles not strategies* on page 33 and then return to lesson four
- Option B is to continue reading the book in chronological order.

Two routes to the same destination – we meet again on page 34.

What is the difference between:

- Knowing and understanding?

- Occupied and engaged?

- Passive and active?

Lesson four

The lesson was based upon a piece of text and a worksheet. A passage from the text and question one on the worksheet are reproduced below:

TEXT   *...the earthquake was caused by movement along the subduction zone.*

QUESTION   *What caused the earthquake?*

ANSWER   *The earthquake was caused by movement along the subduction zone.*

It will come as no great surprise that all thirty children received a tick for their correct answer, while some of them – mostly girls – also received a merit for having written it neatly. It will also come as no great surprise that, when later questioned, only a few of the students had any idea what a subduction zone actually was.

The lesson was due to be repeated the following day with a parallel group. However, on this occasion a small tweak was made and question one now read:

What caused the earthquake? You may NOT use the words subduction, zone or movement in your answer.

It is hard to convey in words the difference between the two lessons. With a single, straightforward tweak, children were now required to actually think and the way in which they responded to the question revealed an enormous amount about their depth of understanding. By simply asking children to *replace* information the emphasis had shifted from children being occupied to children being engaged, from children knowing the answers to understanding them and, most significantly of all, from teaching to learning. What is more, we had our second Magenta Principle.

The experience highlighted two things of significance:

- Much can masquerade as learning; pages of notes, correct answers and being on task can be a convincing disguise
- How a relatively minor change could lead to such a significant switch in emphasis.

It may look similar but there is a fundamental difference between:

A *Read page 7*

and

B *Have a look at page 7 and tell me which you think is the most important sentence.*

Children are simply receiving information in scenario **A**

But in scenario **B** they have to do something to it.

Minor change; major shift

The fact that such a minor change in practice, achieved with a minimum of effort, could lead to such a major shift of emphasis is hugely significant because, put simply, teachers are more likely to make a small adjustment to their practice than a big change. Human beings are creatures of habit, and making a change and more importantly embedding a change takes both time and effort. More than that, teachers by nature are suspicious of gimmicks, initiatives and what they perceive to be unnecessary jargon. They are also largely pragmatic people and very much aware of classroom and behaviour management issues and the implications for planning and preparing lessons.

Perception is crucial; anything that teachers perceive to be manageable, realistic and practical has a far greater chance of being adopted and included in daily practice. For example, there is a significant difference between instructing a group of children to read page 7 and asking them to have a look at page 7 and identify what they believe is the most important sentence. To the superficial glance it may look similar but there has been a fundamental shift in emphasis from children simply receiving information to doing something with it. However, not only are the implications for planning minimal, it is also an exercise that could be completed individually or collaboratively and conducted in silence or used as a catalyst for discussion and debate.

In many respects, the page 7 example above encapsulates what the Magenta Principles are all about. However, it also illustrates a potential caveat; for while reading page 7 and selecting the most important sentence are fundamentally different activities, to the uneducated eye they look just about the same. So many of what we refer to as the Magenta Principles are easy to miss and equally easy to dismiss. Ironically, one of the great positives – i.e. a minor change in practice – can become a negative if people fail to spot the major shift in emphasis that ensues.

There is almost a sub-conscious perception that if the imperative to improve teaching and learning is such an enormous and complex challenge then it can only be met with an equally complex solution. For that reason, it is easy to be seduced into thinking that if it is grand, glossy and expensive then it must be good. Yet complex challenges frequently require simple solutions and it is the little things that can often make the big difference. The worry being that it is all too easy to miss the little things when our eyes are fixed on the big and the obvious.

This book is littered with examples of how teachers have made just a small adjustment to their current practice and have been pleasantly surprised with the impact upon student's learning. Often these have been unplanned and the result of an impromptu question that has challenged a group or a single student to think; a minor, almost unnoticeable change that led to a subtle yet significant change of emphasis.

How do you see your job?

- Help children pass exams?
- Ensure children make progress?
- Help children learn?
- Engage children?
- Excite children?
- Inspire children?
- Have fun?

The challenge was and still is to convince teachers that enjoyment and understanding, and content coverage and examination success, are not mutually exclusive; you can have both and it only requires relatively minor adjustments to practice.

Lessons are for Learning

It was around this time that the profession really began to focus attention upon the centrality of learning and accept that just because the teacher was doing a lot of teaching, it did not necessarily mean the students were doing a lot of learning. We began to acknowledge that learning is an active process involving individuals making personal sense of information and experience. People talked about light-bulb, eureka and penny-dropping moments as teachers gradually started to grasp that there was more to it than children being quiet, doing it neatly and underlining the title with a ruler.

The implication for practice was profound. No longer was the aim of the exercise to transfer the information from text to exercise book so that children could retain and recall it; now we had to help them actually get it. It meant that receiving information was insufficient; in order to understand it students had to do something with it. In short, they had to think about it.

However, despite the rhetoric of learning, a great many teachers saw and still see their job as covering a syllabus and ensuring that students know what they need to know. At worst, they spoon-feed and, to be blunt, pursue examination success at the expense of learning. Of course, knowing can get you a long way; if you know that the earthquake was caused by movement along the subduction zone you will get a tick… and enough ticks will mean that you will pass the exam…and if enough students pass the exam the teacher gets a tick…and if enough teachers get a tick then the school will be get a big tick…

All teachers strive for exam success; everyone has content that needs to be covered and boxes that need to be ticked. However, while some teachers struggle to see beyond this, there are others who want much more. They want their students to both get it and get why they got it so they can get it again tomorrow on their own. They want their students to enjoy their lessons and, at the risk of sounding yucky, be excited and even inspired by their learning. How many geography/maths/art teachers enter the profession because a geography/maths/art teacher inspired them when they were young?

The challenge was and still is to convince teachers that enjoyment and understanding, and content coverage and examination success, are not mutually exclusive; you can have both and it only requires relatively minor adjustments to practice. Whitley Bay High School is a testament to that.

Our job is not to give them **our knowing** but to develop **their** understanding.

Knowing and understanding

Knowing and understanding are both important – the challenge for the teacher is to achieve a healthy balance between the two. A useful starting point – and therefore a worthwhile professional development activity – is to be crystal clear about the difference between them. It sounds a straightforward exercise yet many teachers find it difficult to articulate the difference. Even if teachers struggle to reach a definitive answer, grappling with the question can only be beneficial.

David Perkins, in his excellent book *Smart Schools* provides us with a helpful distinction and suggests that we think of knowing as a state of *possession*, while understanding is a state of *enablement*. Perkins argues that when we understand something, we not only possess certain information but we are enabled to do certain things with that knowledge. He suggests a series of understanding performances or enablement indicators – i.e. the things that an individual can do to demonstrate that they are making the transition from knowing to understanding and moving to a deeper form of learning. For example:

- Explaining something in your own words
- Giving new examples
- Applying new knowledge or skills to different situations
- Justifying something by offering evidence
- Comparing and contrasting
- Contextualising the knowledge
- Creating a metaphor.

There are some obvious parallels with this list and the Magenta Principles on page 39.

If knowing is indeed a state of possession, then it follows that it can be given by someone who has it to someone who doesn't have it. In other words, knowing can be transferred. Understanding, however, cannot be passed between people in the same way – it is done by people, not to them; the product of doing rather than receiving.

There are implications here for the classroom and the role of the teacher. Mark Twain once remarked, *if teaching was as simple as telling we'd all be a lot smarter.* He was right; our job is not to give them our knowing but to develop their understanding, and a model of teaching that is limited to transferring information will simply not suffice.

In order to help teachers reach a deeper understanding of understanding, use the *bookends* technique described on page 169. As you are planning, teaching or observing a lesson, simply ask yourself the question, where is the emphasis – *knowing* or *understanding?*

Look at the examples on the opposite page.

What do you see –

four strategies or one principle?

Principles not strategies

All teachers operate in a specific context. Teaching art is different to teaching maths. Yet all teachers face a common challenge; their job is to help children learn, and learning – deep, meaningful learning – involves individuals making personal sense of information and experience. The teacher who pointed out that he didn't teach maths was right; he teaches children and his job is to engage them and get them thinking in order to make it more likely that they will understand what they are being taught. With that mindset the search is for principles rather than subject-specific strategies and the similarities between teaching maths and art, or primary and secondary, become greater than the differences.

Consider the following:

- A Y4 teacher shows the children the front cover of a previously unseen and unread book. Working in small groups the children are invited to deduce what the story might be about from the front cover alone. The groups are then given three images from the story and challenged to sequence the images in chronological order (see page 56).

- A Y1 teacher shows her class a banana, an avocado, a plum and a kiwi fruit. She first asks the children how many syllables are in each word and then asks them to say the name of each fruit aloud while clapping out the rhythm of the fruit based upon the number of syllables. Each group is then given an envelope containing images of the fruits – three of each. By sequencing the fruits the group can create a rhythm based upon the number of syllables in each word (see page 125).

- A PE is teacher is taking a Y10 group for a trampoline lesson. Each girl is given a pack of cards containing various moves that can be completed on a trampoline such as a front drop or a seat drop. The cards are colour coded to denote a degree of difficulty for each move; for example, some moves such as a seat drop are easier to perform than a somersault. Using the cards the girls have to sequence the moves in order to create a routine.

- A maths teacher is teaching a Y12 group at AS level. Students are issued with a pack of cards and asked to work out the sequence in which the calculations should be performed in order to differentiate a function to find the equation of the tangent (see page 126).

What do you see – four strategies or one principle?

We just asked
the questions:

- What is the principle that underpins the strategy?

- What is the strategy that illustrates the principle?

The wheel existed

A great many teachers will be familiar with some of the approaches in this book, such as the diamond nine activity on page 98, even though they may never have heard of the phrase the Magenta Principles.

It is important to point out that a great many classroom activities, strategies and approaches already existed. It is also important to acknowledge that many excellent resources and ideas have been developed by a huge number of teachers and educationalists over many years.

We did not invent the wheel; nor did we seek to reinvent it. All we sought to do was identify the principle that underpinned an activity and develop a common vocabulary.

For example, we looked at a diamond nine exercise and asked:

- What are children being asked to do with information – what is the theme?
- How can we adapt and develop the idea in a wide variety of contexts – what are the variations on the theme?

So while many schools collected strategies, we set about identifying principles. Indeed, whenever we came across a strategy we endeavored to identify the principle that it was based upon and thought carefully how it could be applied across a range of contexts. It became a two-way process: **What is the principle that underpins the strategy? What is the strategy that illustrates the principle?**

Our thought process was, and indeed still is:

- If it can be done in English, what does it look like in maths?
- If it can be done with text, can it be done with images?
- If it can be done with older students, can it be done with younger children?
- If it can be done with a top set, can it be done with a lower set?
- If it can be done in this order, can it be done the other way around?
- If it can be done at the beginning of a lesson, can it be done at the end?
- If it can be done in a practical subject such as PE, what does it look like in a classroom-based subject?
- If it can be done in a primary school, what does it look like in a secondary school?

The best teachers can think on their feet. Certainly, they plan lessons, but they have plans B, C and D up their sleeve and the confidence and judgement to know when to use them.

Adapt – adopt

We wanted to go further than simply presenting teachers with a collection of 'good ideas'; although there is clearly a place for exposing teachers to a range of teaching strategies, we were wary of teachers adopting techniques without fully understanding the thinking that underpinned them. Being aware of an extensive range of activities may lead to variety, but does not necessarily lead to rich learning experiences; on the contrary, activity for activity's sake is often little more than superficial gloss.

The best teachers can think on their feet. Certainly, they plan lessons, but they have plans B, C and D up their sleeve and the confidence and judgement to know when to use them. For learning – genuine, deep, exciting learning – defies a script or a recipe and while a lesson can be planned in advance, a learning experience most certainly cannot. The best teachers understand this; they know that learning is messy, unstructured and personal and that a prerequisite for facilitating it in others is the ability to respond, adapt and intervene.

Adapting a principle to suit a particular context, subject or circumstance is the hallmark of great teaching and central to the development of the Magenta Principles approach. The ideas in this book therefore are not a collection of strategies to adopt; rather they are a set of principles to adapt. For if we give a teacher a strategy they have a lesson, but if we help them understand the principle…

Principle not principles

Although we ended up with a set of principles, we really ended up with a single, simple rule of thumb; children had to do something with information in order to understand it.

And so the question became: **What do you ask children to do with information in order to make it more likely they will understand it?**

If the answer is receive it, retain it, rehearse it in order to regurgitate it, then it is highly unlikely they will move beyond knowing. They may be on task, they may be doing it neatly and they may even be getting things right – but they are not learning.

If, on the other hand, they are required to interact with, interrogate, manipulate and apply – in short, think about – information, then we open the possibility of children developing a deeper form of understanding. Because we now had the question, we had a vocabulary and the Magenta Principles came along like London buses. Information can be reduced, sequenced, changed, classified, compared, arranged, connected and so on.

What do you ask children to do with information in order to make it more likely they will understand it?

Because we now had the question, we had a vocabulary and the Magenta Principles came along like London buses. Information can be reduced, sequenced, changed, classified, compared, arranged, connected and so on.

A common vocabulary

There is no definitive list, no qualifying criteria and no adjudicator who confers Magenta Principle status. Terminology doesn't matter; making sure classroom practice is effective does. If the phrase proves helpful, please use it; if doesn't, then don't – it is the package, not the packaging, which is important.

And the package is less a list, script, programme or collection of resources and more an approach – even spirit. The common language being a manifestation of a common culture; a philosophy based firmly upon the belief that learning is the product of thinking.

As with any language, there are accents and dialects – for example, some people refer to rank ordering information while others refer to the same practice as prioritising. As long as the local community understands the meaning, the variations around the theme matters little. Similarly, some teachers work around half-a-dozen or so principles, while others make reference to twice that number – the answer to the question *how many magenta principles are there?* being dependent upon the way you answer the question: *what do/could you ask children to do with information in order to make them think?*

In some ways therefore the Magenta Principles are unique to the individual.

However, anyone who recognises the phrase Magenta Principles will be familiar with what are sometimes referred to as the core principles, namely:

reduce	sequence
change	assemble
replace	classify
add	compare
arrange	connect

Others may be added to the list: enlarge, simplify, exaggerate, collect, prioritise, share; while some – those who take learning to another level – would also include reconcile.

There is no mystery – they do what they say on the tin. Arrange simply means that students are required to arrange information!

The Magenta Principles are not ready-meals.

Put simply, two teachers, same Magenta Principle and the result will be variable amounts of learning.

Illustrating the Magenta Principles

There are two types of shop; some are highly organised and clearly labelled with a discrete aisle devoted to bathroom appliances, one for kitchenware and so on. These shops are hugely efficient and you can quickly and easily locate precisely what you are looking for.

Then there are those shops that are cluttered, chaotic and crammed to the gunwales with seemingly unrelated items. There appears to be neither rhyme nor reason behind the layout. You don't really know what you are looking for but they look interesting so you have a wander around, rummage away and, before you know it, uncover a little gem.

This section resembles the latter shop. Come on in and have a browse. You may not know exactly what you are looking for, or precisely where to look, but you'll know when you see it.

Warning

Before you enter make sure you notice the warning sign above the door pointing out that the Magenta Principles are not a panacea – neither, as I prefer to make the point, are they ready-meals. They are simply the catalyst for thinking and talking; the extent and depth of the learning that takes place is largely dependent upon the way the process is mediated and facilitated by the teacher. **Put simply, two teachers, same Magenta Principle, and the result will be variable amounts of learning.**

Later in the book, the Magenta Principles are likened to the fabric of a tent; of little use without the support and structure provided by the poles. Two dimensions in particular – the tent poles – are central to the Magenta Principles approach:

- Facilitation
- Consolidation.

To fully understand the Magenta Principles it is important to be aware of both a range of ideas and activities *and* be able to fully grasp the crucial role played by facilitation and consolidation in the approach – the dilemma being which to cover first. The choice is again left to the reader; skip ahead a read pages 147-163 or continue reading in chronological order.

Example one: PE – reduce

It was a badminton lesson. The first player hit a long overhead clear (hit the shuttle a long way) and when his opponent was stranded at the back of the court, followed up by playing a delicate drop shot.

At that point I intervened and posed the question, *which shot won the point?*

Both boys immediately replied the drop shot. I paused and, after a few seconds, one of the boys suddenly said *but you wouldn't be able to play a drop shot if you hadn't first played the overhead clear.*

I smiled and repeated the original question, *so which shot won the point?*

Michael Kelly
PE teacher

Example two: maths – connect and reduce

My Y12 group has been studying trigonometric identities and has reached a point where they are required to use a variety of these to simplify expressions and equations. Many of the class were struggling to know which equations they could use and at which time. Whilst recognising when to use equations in their original form students were struggling to notice how these equations could be manipulated and used in different settings.

For non-mathematicians, the key point here is that many of them are rearranged versions of each other, so students only need to remember a few key equations and that the rest can be derived from these few. This task was devised in order to deepen their understanding. Initially, students were given a pack of equation cards (below). These cards contained a number of equations that are simple manipulations of each other.

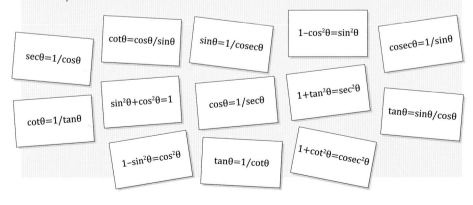

$\sec\theta = 1/\cos\theta$

$\cot\theta = \cos\theta/\sin\theta$

$\sin\theta = 1/\csc\theta$

$1 - \cos^2\theta = \sin^2\theta$

$\csc\theta = 1/\sin\theta$

$\cot\theta = 1/\tan\theta$

$\sin^2\theta + \cos^2\theta = 1$

$\cos\theta = 1/\sec\theta$

$1 + \tan^2\theta = \sec^2\theta$

$\tan\theta = \sin\theta/\cos\theta$

$1 - \sin^2\theta = \cos^2\theta$

$\tan\theta = 1/\cot\theta$

$1 + \cot^2\theta = \csc^2\theta$

Task one: The first task was to **connect** cards together that they felt were linked. Students were guided to complete an A3 sheet where they wrote down which equations they felt were connected and why. At this point students were beginning to notice that whilst all appeared to be different, a number of the cards were showing similar information.

At this point I started to hear comments from students such as *both derived from sin²x+cos²x, they're all rearrangements of each other* and *they are a rearranged formula of the original identity.*

Task two: The students were then asked to **reduce** their initial pack of cards to a core few which they would then have to memorise. Students used the connections they had made in the previous task to decide which cards they could omit. Comments from students at this point included *these are the core identities which can be manipulated to form the other identities* and *I have ignored all rearrangements.*

Students were then asked to hide any cards that did not make the final reduced pack.

Task three: Finally, they were then asked to **expand** on the equations by manipulating them to create the other equations that didn't make the cut. After some work students started to realise that as long as they could remember a few core equations they could derive any other equations they might need. Students again wrote down their methods for expanding; however, this time they were asked how doing this task had helped their understanding of trig equations.

Their comments included *it has demonstrated that all the identities can be derived from each of the basic functions* and *this has helped me because it makes you expand the formulas into all the different types.*

In lessons since this task students have showed they have a much deeper understanding of trigonometry and are no longer looking through their books to find the exact identity they need to solve a problem. Students seem much keener to look for a deeper understanding of the subject rather than simply rote learn the identities that they require.

Chris Johnson
Whitley Bay High School

Example three: primary – add

Children in a Y 1/2 mixed class had chosen the rainforest as their topic focus for the term. They wanted to find out about the different layers of the rainforest and which animals lived in/on each layer. The children carried out some research using books and computers and we also watched some video clips. Following on from this, we discussed the fact that there could be many animals and plants still undiscovered in the rainforests of the world. The children were then encouraged to imagine that they had explored an area of the rainforest and discovered a new animal. They had to decide which of the layers this animal lived in and then draw it. They then labelled it as to the features common to the sorts of animals already living in this layer.

I wanted the activity we undertook to mean that the children could demonstrate the depth of their understanding in a way that they would enjoy and that would mean the children would still recall what they had discovered and learned weeks, hopefully months, afterwards.

The activity definitely sparked the children's interest and I had reports from parents who commented upon how the children had come home enthused by the day's learning and able to share what they had found out. Most importantly, they all clearly demonstrated that they understood that animals with different attributes can be found in different areas of the rainforest. Two terms on, we have a topic, again chosen by the children, called 'Beasts and Botany'; the children, when undertaking some learning about mini beasts, became very excited – recalling the rainforest learning – and asked if they could 'design' a new insect!

Emma Johns
Sidmouth CE Primary School

Example four: Maths – change

There are many variations on this activity but the basic idea is use a graph drawing package, which, when you type in an equation, will draw the graph.

One of my favourite exercises is to show students how to make a circle by using the equation $x^2 + y^2 = 16$ and then challenging them to make the best possible face.

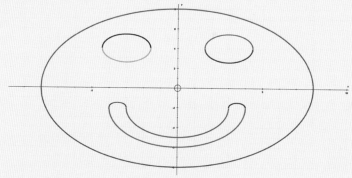

This face was produced by a Y11 student using semi-circles starting with the equation $y = (64 - x^2)^{1/2}$ and then using graphical transformations.

The activity encourages students to experiment with equations and discover the connection between the changes to the equation and the changes to the graph. They can then develop the ability to decide what they want the graph to look like and work out the equation that is required.

Tom Walton
The Ecclesbourne School

Example five: Humanities – replace

Define spiritual emptiness (gwacter ysbrydol) without using the words gwag (empty) and ysbryd (spirit).

The answer I had was one of the best definitions I've heard this term – *Mae fel petai eich tu fewn wedi'ch gadael chi*, or in English, *It's as if your inside has left you.*

Rachel Nicholson
Ysgol Bro Dinefwr, Llandeilo

Example six: MFL – assemble

I used this activity with my Y10 group. The idea was that students had to select one word/phrase from each column to assemble a phrase that makes sense in French. For the benefit of non-linguists, there is only one correct way that the phrases go together to make sense! For example, beginning in the top left-hand corner with the words *oui, j'ai*. They then have to choose the correct word from the second column that is the only one that will fit accurately with that word. In this case it would be *fait un*, then the next *stage dans* and finally *une école maternelle*.

Est-ce que tu as fait un stage?

* Challenge

Oui, j'ai	une	stage dans	garage
J'ai passé	pas fait	dans un cabinet	de vétérinaire
Mon stage	fait un	un stage cette	une école maternelle
Je n'ai	a été	semaine dans un	année

** Challenge

il	dû classer	faire	téléphone
elles	a	les	au téléphone
vous	ont dû prendre	dû répondre au	des photocopies
Nous avons	avez dû	des commandes	fiches

*** Challenge – create your own mixture of both * and **

This is one of my favorite Magenta Principles exercises that we use in MFL because it is the catalyst for such valuable discussion – not only that, it is a really challenging task and students have to draw on their understanding in order to complete it. Students work in pairs and are asked to think aloud as they do it. Student dialogue is ripe and leads to discussions such as *no, it has to have the negative bit...that sandwich thing she talks about ...the ne and the pas with the filling the verb in the middle.*

The activity is easily differentiated as students can decide on their own starting point. The second set of words are harder due to the fact that verb formation comes into play but also the fact that there is a greater breakdown, which really fine-tunes their thinking and grammar awareness. The final activity is really challenging and again gets students to discuss how they can produce their own version of the activity for someone else in the group. By creating this in pairs they have to ensure that it fits accordingly and again the discussion is really focused on the understanding of the language.

It is one of those exercises that requires minimal planning but is really effective at generating dialogue.

Suzanne McArdle
Trinity School, Carlisle

Example seven: primary – connect

I gave each child in my Y2 class a bingo sheet with six assorted characters from traditional stories. The aim was to improve understanding of adjectives and how they add to our understanding of character.

I read out an adjective – e.g. selfish, clever, greedy, generous and so on – and the children put their counter on the character they thought matched the adjective. When questioned, they had to be able to tell me why that word matched that character and then I opened their explanation to the class and asked them if they agreed or disagreed, did they have a different character they thought matched the adjective and so on.

All the children were involved and all were enthusiastic from the highest to the lowest ability. As an extension, the children were able to reuse their sheet by creating their own adjective word bank to play again independently. It was a brilliant start to a lesson as it got them all thinking, connecting ideas and talking!!

Rachel Hayward
Y2/3 teacher

Example eight: primary – change/connect

My Y5/6 class had been introduced to the concept of art and music that appeared abstract and unrelated to their own life experiences. Through discussion about social climate at the time of construction/composition, the beliefs of the artist and the emotions they wished to convey, the children were able to see that these may be reflected through the artwork/music but they were also allowed to overlay them with their own individual experiences and beliefs. Basically, that there was no absolute interpretation of a piece of music or artwork…their opinions only added to the overall impact it had.

I posed them the question, *if the artist Miro had been a chef, what would have been on his menu and why?*

I later followed this up by asking them to consider how the menu for his early works would change in his later works. Immediately, the students started thinking a lot deeper about artistic traits, techniques, social impacts, influences and the worth in the opinions of others and themselves.

One child, while looking at one of Miro's first masterpieces, *L'Oiseau lune jaune/Yellow moonbird* (below), claimed:

This is a sad meal…one egg on a plate being made to last as the spoon drags it around the plate to make it last longer. I think Miro is saying a starving world can't be fed by any chef if there is not enough food.

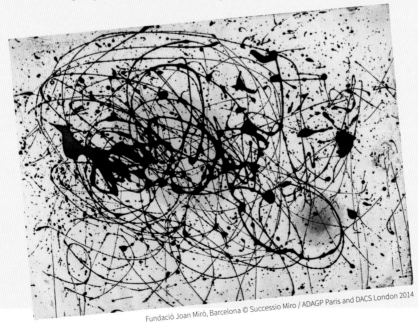

Fundació Joan Miró, Barcelona © Successio Miro / ADAGP Paris and DACS London 2014

To conclude, this activity allowed all the children within this mixed ability, multicultural, mixed gender class to not only learn about an artist and his skills but to also recognise that they had a relevant and meaningful opinion which could not be wrong. These were not pictures they would have felt they could interpret or relate to, but this misconception was challenged and this led to an improvement in self-confidence and self-worth. All felt part of the class team, all felt heard, all felt safe enough to think outside the box. As one child said *I get it now…I can understand things I don't understand at first if I just think about them differently!*

Liz Webster
Yenton Primary School, Erdington

Example nine: English – reduce/enlarge

Before reading a new novel (*Trash* by Andy Mulligan) I gave my Y9 group eight key words from the blurb on the back cover.

Dumpsite	Mysterious	Map	Corruption
Key	Mountains	Police	Violence

I then gave them just five minutes to transform these into a 50–150 word mini story. We then compared what they had come up with to the blurb. It was interesting to see how close some of their ideas were. It led to a good discussion about likely themes and ideas in the novel, as well as how vocabulary can produce a mood/atmosphere/genre. We then prioritised the order of the key words as a prediction task: which words might best sum up what will happen in the novel?

The idea for this activity was totally impromptu. I was in the library with a bottom Y7 set and there were about 10 minutes of the lesson left. They had all just selected a new book to read so I asked them to look at the blurb on the back cover and to select what they considered to be the key words. From the key words I asked them to predict what they thought the book was going to be about. It really got them talking and thinking and worked so well that I decided to turn it into a full-blown activity and use it with my Y9 set.

Layla Hill
Wymondham High Academy

Example ten: English – reduce/search/change

I wanted to prepare pupils for an exam where they have to analyse an extract of unseen prose. Attacking a text thoroughly and swiftly was the aim so I wanted pupils to learn the strategies they would need to have up their sleeves and, most importantly, be able to take these away with them to apply to other texts. In this lesson I gave them Vol. 2 Chapter 1 from *Wuthering Heights* where Cathy is dying and has her last dramatic moments with Heathcliff.

At the planning stage I decided to try applying several of the Magenta Principles to the text. Pupils began by reading and reducing the chapter to key quotations. Then I asked them in groups to prioritise the key quotations before reducing them to just three, to give a flavour of the passage. Of course, this led to pupils having to negotiate, explain and justify their choices. After this introduction to the extract, we moved on to some of the more unusual Magenta Principles. These created lots of interesting discussion, enthusiasm (especially for period 6!) and thought-provoking comments. Pupils agreed that they had enjoyed it, felt confident with the extract and, most importantly, could take away some of the tasks to help them with their own revision. I will definitely be using the same strategy and tasks across other texts and year groups.

Some of the most interesting uses of the Magenta Principles were:

Search for all the exclamation marks and question marks. Of course this was simple, but once we had discussed the effect on the rhythm and mood of the passage and the effect on characterisation it led to a fantastic comment: *Cathy's all about the exclamation marks isn't she, Miss? You wouldn't get Jane Eyre using those. She's more of a semi-colon person.* When pushed to expand... *she wouldn't allow her emotions to run away with her like that – she's too poised and measured.* This was delightful, and they were off, talking about which punctuation marks other characters would be and why.

Changing Cathy and Heathcliff's relationship to a symbol or a colour (I gave the choice) created much enthusiasm and led to some inspired ideas. One group decided on a caduceus (a wand entwined with two snakes) to show the way they nurture and depend on one another and the characters' associations with hell. Another chose a thorny rose, but it was green to show their jealousy and reflect the nature of the imagery used to describe their love. Again, these were **expanded** into interesting discussions about the novel and finding textual evidence.

I found this a really energetic, colourful and fun lesson and easy to plan because I just created a task for several of the principles and let things happen. We seemed to cover lots of ground as the pace was fast and the unusual tasks created buzz. Frequently, I could just stand back and let the discussions unfold, giving a great opportunity to assess understanding and intervene only to move things on.

Layla Hill
Wymondham High Academy

Example eleven: science – change

It was a Y10 lesson that I had taught many times on natural selection. The key challenge is for the students to remember the steps involved in natural selection – variation, competition, survival, inheritance and evolution – in the correct order so they can apply them to another context. However, they often get confused – not least because they struggle to remember the correct order of the steps. I was looking for a way of making the lesson more interactive so the students could better understand the content.

The basic idea was to attach a physical gesture or action to each of the five steps. Initially, they worked in groups before we decided as a class which of the gestures best represented each step. For example, we decided that a flurry of punches to mimic a fight was a good way to symbolise competition, a V for victory sign would remind us of the V for variation and we rubbed our fingers together as if we had just come into money to represent inheritance. We then proceeded to apply these steps when considering how an ancestral penguin had evolved into a modern day gentoo.

At the end of the unit test the students were faced with a similar question regarding the evolution of tortoises. In years gone by students would often pick up one or two marks on this type of question but students in this group were picking up five and six marks. It was a noticeable improvement; not only did they remember it far better they were also able to apply it.

Emma Joyce
Trinity School, Carlisle

Example twelve: primary – arrange/change

To start our work on bees I decided to have a target board with lots of statements about bees on it. The class (mixed FDN/Y1) worked in small groups and arranged the statements on the target board going from fact to fiction.

Bees wear stripy jumpers

Bees eat jelly

Bees will always sting you

Bees can cry

Bees can talk to each other

Bees live together in houses

Bees work together

Bees make honey

Bees have wings

Bees collect pollen

Bees eat flowers

This not only created discussion but I was able to assess how much they already knew about the topic. We then reviewed the target board at the end of the topic and were able to know all the answers and move some of statements that we had not known.

I then asked the children to role-play a bee (in a previous lesson on body parts the children had made bee finger puppets). The children were put into hives (teams); we discussed which bees did what and that they were going to be the worker bees collecting pollen. Around the room were lots of pots with flowers on them (made by the children) and in the pots were crushed-up Wotsits. The children were then given a time limit to collect as much 'pollen' as they could from the flowers and bring it back to the hive. Children stuck their finger in the pot and got little bits of 'pollen' on their fingers.

The children **LOVED** the lesson; not only were they all engaged and excited but they also were able to understand how a bee collects pollen and how bees work together.

Meryl Logan
Sidmouth CE Primary School

Example thirteen: RE – change

This lesson involved using Play-Doh to create a physical representation of the Holy Spirit. It was inspired by my then young children Jessica and Daniel, who had used Play-Doh to create the main character from a story that I had made up for them the night before.

The concept of God and in particular the Holy Spirit is not an easy one for children to understand. The purpose of this activity was for pupils to take an abstract concept and turn it into something concrete that had meaning for them.

Examples included:

- A tightrope with a model person walking along it, with a safety net underneath it to represent God/the Holy Spirit.
- A person (representing humanity) walking along with a large hand behind him representing God/the Holy Spirit guiding them, ready to catch them when they fall.
- A lion to represent God's strength.

One of the students commented: *I made footprints out of Play-Doh. I saw God as this because we can follow him and his way of life, yet like some footprints, we don't know exactly what the thing that made them is. This helped me understand what I thought about God without worrying what other people thought – nothing was wrong and I could understand why other people saw God as a different thing.*

The use of Play-Doh has allowed me to assess pupils' understanding by seeing the end product but equally as important, their explanation of what they had created, why, and what it meant to them. Every time I teach this lesson, I am both humbled and amazed at the sculptures and the meaning they hold for the pupils and how much they actually progress as a result of the lesson. It allows a depth of learning that could not possibly be achieved by text and teacher-led teaching alone. The spiritual development taking place is almost tangible in itself.

Rebecca Burton
St Augustine's RC High School, Billington

Example fourteen: History – assemble/arrange

It was the beginning of a new piece of work and I decided to frame the entire unit around a big question:

Who was responsible for the death of Sir Thomas More?

At the time most students didn't even know who Sir Thomas More was!

Step one: I arranged the students into groups of six and asked them to deal out their pack of clue cards. The rule was that no one could show anyone else what was written on their cards but they were allowed to read them out.

Some of the cards were simply factual:

Others provided a bit more in the way of detail:

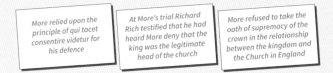

While others were deliberately designed to spread a bit of confusion and make students think:

This exercise sparked off a large amount of discussion but was deliberately designed to generate as many questions as it provided answers.

Step two: The group were issued with character cards: Sir Thomas More, Henry VIII, the Pope, Thomas Cromwell, Richard Rich, Ann Boleyn, Catherine Howard. In addition, they received two blank character cards.

They were then asked to respond to the question *who was responsible for the death of Sir Thomas More?* by arranging their character cards in a diamond nine (see page 98). It was stressed that this was no more than a first go using the limited information they had and that they would have a chance of revisiting the activity a little later.

I wasn't expecting them to be able to complete the diamond nine exercise at this stage but it certainly – as was the intention – got them thinking and talking. It also provided me with an insight into what was going on in their minds.

Step three: I had set up six stations that contained additional information about aspects of the topic. For example, one station contained information about the oath of supremacy, one contained information about the trial of Sir Thomas More, one contained information about the principle of *qui tacet consentire videtur* and so on. One person from each group was sent to each station where they had an opportunity to find out more detailed information.

Step four: The original groups reconvened and were invited to reconsider their diamond nine in the light of the new information.

Step five: Each group was allowed to ask me one question. This was delivered to me in a sealed envelope so that they couldn't hear what the other groups were talking about.

Step six: The groups completed their diamond nine activity and were asked to speak for two minutes to justify the character they thought was most responsible for Thomas More's death.

Step seven: As most groups had concluded more than one person bore some responsibility for the death of Sir Thomas More, I asked each student to produce a blame cake (left) with a paragraph to justify their blame cake for homework.

The brilliant aspect to this lesson was watching how the student's understanding developed almost layer by layer at the various stages of the task. There is no doubt that by framing the lesson as an investigation into a big question and by encouraging students to grapple with the clues they developed a much deeper appreciation of the issue – much deeper than if I had just imparted the information myself.

Ellie Hughes
History teacher

Image **A**

© *Grandmother's Song* by Barbara Soros Illustrated by Jackie Morris

Example fifteen: Primary English – sequence

When introducing a new text to the class I often begin by presenting them with the cover and some images from the book in order to get them thinking about the possible content. On this particular occasion I was looking at the book *The Grandmother's Song* by Barbara Soros. It is a fantastic book and ideal for this kind of activity.

Step one: I split the class into small groups and gave them the front cover of the book. The task was to use the clues in the picture to see if they could predict what the story was about. In particular, I asked them which country they thought the book was set in and why.

Image **C**

Step two: I gave the groups three images from the story (opposite) and asked them to sequence them into the order in which they thought the images appeared in the book. I also asked them to use the images to try to work out what was happening in the story. For children so young there were some profound ideas about the people in the pictures fleeing a war, leaving to find more food because there wasn't any left near their home and about the relationships between the people in the images.

Step three: I then told the children that the first sentence from the book was:

In the heart of Mexico, hawks soar above high mountains and swoop down to the gentle slopes of corn below.

I then issued them with three other pieces of text from the book – one of which was the last sentence of the book.

A *This is my gift I am stroking into you. It is also the gift of my grandmother and her grandmother before her.*

B *No matter where we are grandmother is never far away. And whenever we need her we can simply shut our eyes and feel her holding us so very close.*

C *She held the humming-bird with the same tenderness as her grandmother had held her and carried it inside.*

They had to consider how the text fitted with what they thought would happen in the story and were allowed to change the order in which they had placed the images if they wished. They were also asked to identify which piece of text, A, B or C, was the actual last sentence.

The activities really got the children thinking and there was a huge amount of discussion. My role was largely to ask *why* and encourage the children to explain their thinking and justify their answers. I thoroughly enjoyed teaching this lesson and the children thoroughly enjoyed the activity. In particular they liked the fact that they could not be wrong and so were happy to join in and contribute ideas. The TA in the classroom commented on how engaged the children were and noted that even those that sometimes found literacy lessons difficult made really valuable contributions.

Gina Bedford
Pinders Primary School, Wakefield

Answers on page 216

The lessons described at the beginning of the book – the English lesson based upon the question who was the key character and the geography lesson that required students to reduce a piece of text to the six key words – are hardly earth shattering. Rather, they are simple and straightforward ideas that are manageable, realistic and require only a minor adjustment to classroom practice. Yet simple can be effective; very effective, for we have switched the emphasis from occupied to engaged, passive to active, teaching to learning.

Unpacking the Magenta Principles

Reference has already been made to the challenge faced when writing this book, for while describing the task is relatively straightforward it is infinitely more difficult to capture and convey the experience. It is the difference between looking at a map of the London Underground and travelling on it. However, in order to adapt the Magenta Principles and develop them in the context of your classroom it is important to get under the skin of them and fully understand the approach. With that aim in mind, therefore, let us explore the examples on pages 42-57 in a little more depth. What did you see when you read through them – a collection of activities or an underpinning philosophy?

Arguably, the example that best encapsulates the Magenta Principles approach is example one, when the PE teacher poses the simple question, *which shot won the point?* That choice will no doubt raise an eyebrow or two and leave some people – those who equate excellence with *all singing and dancing* – feeling a little underwhelmed. Certainly, there are more eye-catching and innovative examples, but the Magenta Principles are not about singing and dancing, they are about learning and challenging children to think. In this particular lesson the teacher does just that; not by using Post-its, Play-Doh or PowerPoint but by posing a solitary question. Had they not done so they would have missed a valuable opportunity to take the learning a little bit deeper and a little bit further.

That is not to say that the many imaginative and novel activities in this book are ineffective. On the contrary, there are some wonderful examples of innovative, even inspiring, lessons that achieve the twin objective of lessons that both engage and excite. The point is that they are excellent lessons because they are effective, not simply because they are a bit different.

The significance of the badminton lesson lies in the fact that it is a routine, bread and butter lesson that did not require overlengthy planning and resourcing. By simply posing the unplanned, impromptu question – which shot won the point? – the teacher challenged the students to think. It is no coincidence that the phrase *challenged the students to think* has been used on more than one occasion on this page, for the Magenta Principles are not a collection of activities, no matter how innovative, but a pedagogy based upon the unshakeable belief that learning is the consequence of thinking.

- *In lessons since this task students have showed they have a much deeper understanding*
- I had reports from parents who commented upon how the children had come home enthused by the day's learning
- *The exercise really got them talking and thinking*
- This enabled me to assess where they were in terms of understanding and intervene as and when required
- *This is one of my favorite Magenta Principles exercises that we use in MFL because it is the catalyst for such valuable discussion…*
- …not only that, it is a really challenging task and students have to draw on their understanding in order to complete it
- *The activity is easily differentiated*
- It is one of those exercises that requires minimal planning but is really effective at generating dialogue
- *The aim was to improve understanding*
- It got them all thinking, connecting ideas and talking!
- *The idea for this activity was totally impromptu*
- Not only were they all engaged and excited but they also were able to understand
- *As one child said 'I get it now…I can understand things I don't understand at first if I just think about them differently!'*
- It allows a depth of learning that could not possibly be achieved by text and teacher-led teaching alone
- *In years gone by students would often pick up one or two marks on this type of question but students in this group were picking up five and six marks. It was a noticeable improvement*
- The children **LOVED** the lesson

Mindset

In the Foreword, Adam Chedburn makes reference to the moment when the Cheshire Cat suggests to Alice that the direction she should take depends upon where she wants to get to. Where do you want to get to and what do you hope to achieve are not bad questions to start with, and if the answer to both is learning then the direction is obvious.

The Magenta Principles are a mindset; a mindset that says my role is to help children learn. And if learning – not teaching – is the focus, the questions are obvious: How do I make this interesting? How do I enthuse them? How do I make this memorable? How do I make them think? How do I get them talking? How do I help them get it? Or, in a nutshell, the question that should be on every teacher's lips as they plan a lesson; **what am I asking them to do to/with information?**

Rooted in learning

In 1997 I nailed my colours to the mast and suggested that *Lessons are for Learning*. Both mast and nail were strong, for my colours remain firmly in place; learning is our focus. If that is accepted, then *how is this helping them learn?* has to be the question and if we cannot answer it, then we quite simply shouldn't be doing it; for pedagogy should not be driven by curriculum coverage, assessment structures, inspection frameworks or politics but informed by what we know about learning and the learning process. It is as true today as it was yesterday and will be tomorrow.

The Magenta Principles are effective because they are rooted in learning. Indeed, if we were drawing a Magenta Principle family tree, then there is no doubt that the parents at the top of the diagram would be *change* and *connect*. For change and connect – arguably the two most important principles – are central to the way in which human beings learn and develop understanding. Learning involves individuals making personal sense of information, or, in other words, creating meaning. They do this by making connections between new information and experiences with existing knowledge; it is a simple matter of biology.

> The Magenta Principles focus my understanding of learning. Instead of thinking *how am I going to teach this?*, I find myself thinking *how are pupils going to learn this?* I have a toolkit of practical active learning strategies, which sets the pupil at the heart of the learning process and the results are phenomenal.
>
> Gemma Gilbert
> *English teacher*

Sandwich technique

Step one: begin the lesson with a question or activity.

Step two: continue the lesson with activities, discussion and so on.

Step three: end the lesson with the same question/activity you began with.

The difference in their answer from the beginning to the end is an indication of how their understanding has developed and how much progress they have made.

New learning

There are two broad ways in which a teacher can help students develop understanding:

- The teacher can teach something – explain, show, model and so on – and then let the students have a go.
- The teacher can allow the student to have a go – explore, manipulate, speculate, infer – and then help them draw out and consolidate their learning.

It should be stressed that both approaches are valid and have a place; there is no suggestion that children have to find out everything for themselves. However, it is equally important to point out that learning is not dependent upon teachers telling and that children cannot find things out for themselves.

The Magenta Principles are more than a collection of activities that enable children to practise what they have just been taught; they are an effective way of introducing children to new learning. Example fourteen – *who was responsible for the death of Sir Thomas More?* – is an illustration of this approach. The students had no prior knowledge of Sir Thomas More before the lesson but by exploring the issue – to be precise, assembling and arranging information – they began to develop an appreciation of the events that surrounded his execution. Indeed, the teacher makes reference to watching how the students' understanding developed almost layer by layer at the various stages of the task and suggests that they developed a much deeper appreciation of the issue – *much deeper than if I had just imparted the information myself.*

That is not to say that the teacher doesn't do anything. On the contrary, their role and the way in which they listen, intervene and facilitate is crucial and will help children go further than they would have gone alone. The significant point, however, is that the teacher doesn't always have to go first.

Sandwich technique

This involves deliberately using the same task, or question, more than once during the lesson or unit of work in order to gauge how a student's understanding has developed. For example, students completed the diamond nine activity regarding the death of Sir Thomas More at the beginning of the lesson and then revisited the same activity towards the end of the lesson when they had been exposed to additional information. Our aim must always be that they leave the room knowing more than when they entered, and this approach – known as the sandwich technique – is a clear indicator of where they were at the beginning and where they are at the end.

Our mindset must be:

- If it can be done in maths what does it look like in English?

- If it works with older students how can it be adapted to suit younger children?

- If it can be done with text can it be done with images?

- Would it work the other way around?

- How could I adapt and develop this idea?

- Create a set of name cards bearing the child's SIMS photo. Add a coloured border for the purposes of differentiation based on any appropriate filter – for example, learning dispositions: yellow borders for reluctant speakers, red for confident leaders, green for ideas generators, orange for good researchers and so on. The teacher can move the students with green borders round the groups to build up the ideas bank, or get the students with yellow borders to take on the role of group scribe so that they can give oral feedback to the class based on notes they have taken themselves – thus increasing their confidence to speak aloud.

Secret number 3: Embed the name cards in the fabric of your planning.

- Name cards mean that the teacher indisputably determines who sits where in a classroom – *I've seated you in these places for your learning.* Children never sit in the same seat for more than three consecutive lessons at WBHS so they do not become territorial. Disruptive behaviour is eliminated because students are placed in their most productive pairs and fours. Children like boundaries that are fair and visible: name cards evidence that.
- Each seating plan is directly linked to the aims of the lesson, the strategies to be used and the ability of each student. Everyone in the room is supporting the learning of others: high ability pairs may work together opposite lower ability partners; good questioners can be paired with reflective individuals; spontaneity can be partnered with caution – the possibilities are endless but all give scope for students to make meaning for themselves.
- Name cards promote equal opportunities. If it's true that there is no single word more important in any language than your own name, then every child's individuality has been recognised.

> Of course you think at first that you want to sit where you like, but the advantage of name cards is that you come across a wide range of different points of view which helps broaden your thinking and challenges you to question your opinions. At the same time you make friends with people you wouldn't necessarily get to know otherwise.
>
> Ellie Lee
> *Year 13 Student, Whitley Bay High School*

Summary

- Adopt a left page/ right page format for textbooks

- Use a Magenta Principles dice

- Teach students ABOUT the Magenta Principles

Main content

Magenta dice

At Whitley Bay High School we have used *magenta dice* in conjunction with the Left Hand – Right Hand page idea to challenge the students to try out the different principles. Each face of the dice has a different magenta-influenced task on it, for example, *reduce your notes to one sentence* or *change your text into a summary diagram*. When the discussion has finished and students have taken notes on the right hand page, they roll the dice and then complete the task that fate has selected for them on the left hand page. This random selection means the students are less able to rely solely on one, comfortable principle but rather have to process the information in a variety of ways.

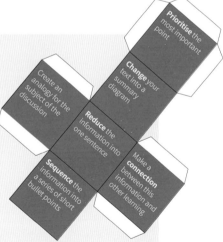

Alan Keegan
Whitley Bay High School

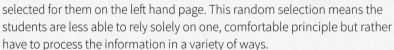

Maths – reduce

The basic idea of this activity is to challenge students to try the most difficult question. It is a variation of *do the three hardest* and is based upon the TV quiz show *Pointless*.

The students are shown a set of questions (for example, the questions below) and are challenged to answer correctly the most difficult one they can. As the questions become increasingly difficult so the marks awarded for answering them decrease with the hardest question being worth zero marks. The aim of the exercise is to be pointless. **Answers overleaf**

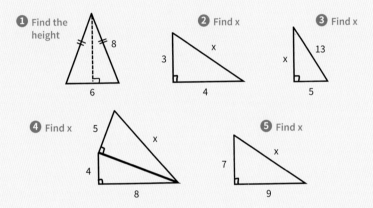

Pointless maths is very effective for revision. It works well in teams and the competitive element will encourage students to try difficult questions they might otherwise shy away from.

The most effective use of this idea to date has been for gradually introducing new mathematical techniques. For example, having taught the class the general idea of Pythagoras's theorem we used pointless to introduce how to find a shorter side and then how to use the theorem to solve problems. It was quick and simple but very motivational as students wanted to know how to answer the more difficult questions so that they could get fewer points in the next round!

I particularly love the discussion it provokes about which is the most difficult question – especially when the class disagree with me!

Tom Walton
The Ecclesbourne School

Answers to previous page

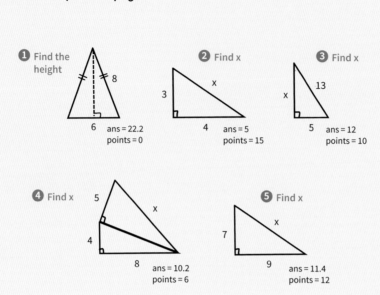

1 Find the height

8

6   ans = 22.2
points = 0

2 Find x

x

3

4   ans = 5
points = 15

3 Find x

13

x

5   ans = 12
points = 10

4 Find x   5

x

4

8   ans = 10.2
points = 6

5 Find x

x

7

9   ans = 11.4
points = 12

Primary – reduce

I invited my Y4 class to explore as many different ways to roll as possible. I then asked them to reduce their rolls down to two – the hardest and the easiest.

The activity was highly successful. It made them think seriously about the rolls, and the discussion that ensued was great. Lots of *I think this is harder, because…No this is harder, because…* I particularly liked the comment *my head gets in the way of rolling backwards. If you could just remove it you would roll backwards easily!*

Leah Stratton
Sidmouth CE Primary School

As my Year 7 class had been learning about ostinato and chords, I presented them with a range of different chords – in the form of diagrams – for a range of instruments and a series of repeating melodies using staff notation. The class had to incorporate these into their music compositions. In order to begin higher order thinking, I simply asked, *which chord and which melody do you think is the hardest?* This enabled them to understand why certain chords and melodies are harder to play; possibly because of different rhythms, more notes and so on, which led onto further discussions and demonstrations.

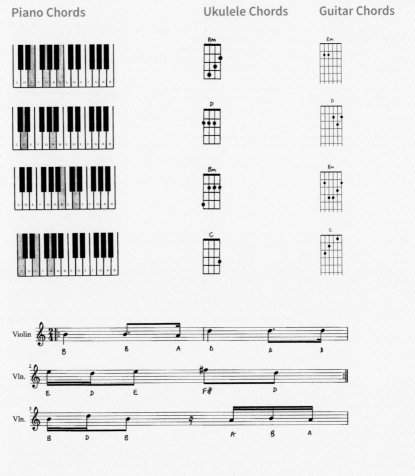

Piano Chords   **Ukulele Chords**   **Guitar Chords**

Sarah Doe
Chiltern Training Group

Performing Arts – reduce

The task for my Y12 BTEC Performing Arts class was to devise a short drama that experiments with the use of tension. However, students were only allowed to use a maximum of 10 words and a time limit of three minutes.

Initially, students thought that this would be a straightforward activity. However, it actually presented them with a real challenge as they often rely on the spoken work in drama as the main form of communication. The activity was highly successful not only in terms of getting students to focus on the physicality of their performance as a way of communicating with an audience, but also in terms of understanding Pinter's style of theatre.

Sara Raywood
Lutterworth College

Maths – reduce

Each pupil is asked to provide a summary of a section or topic of work – for example, Pythagoras, trigonometry, analysing data and so on – that is limited to a maximum of two pages of A4. The aim is to help students get to the heart of a topic.

Students then use these summaries to answer a series of problems. This will enable the student to test whether their summary is any good. They then have a chance to improve and update them in light of this.

These summaries then form the basis of their own *Pupil Revision Folder*, which develops over the period of their GCSE course culminating in their unique and personal *Revision Guide*. From time to time students swap summaries and use somebody else's notes to tackle a series of problems. Students then provide critical feedback to their peers and the summaries are further improved on the good and bad aspects in light of this very useful feedback.

There is no doubt that this process has resulted in vastly improved mathematical communication skills and a deeper understanding of the subject. Some of the pupil summaries could easily compete with those that are currently for sale in the market at present!

Tony Purkiss
All Saints School, Dagenham

Technology – reduce

When we mark work it is usual to give students three G comments and an I comment (the G stands for good and highlights things they have done well and the I denotes an aspect of the work that could be improved).

I asked the students if they only received one comment on their work, would they rather have a G or an I?

What a fascinating discussion!

Andrew Palmer
Trinity School, Carlisle

PE – reduce

Following a cross-country run which had been completed quicker than anticipated I found I had a little unexpected time on my hands.

Step one: I asked the question, *which had been the most important few minutes of the run?* Was it:

1 The first minute?	*3* The uphill section?	*5* The warm-up?
2 The last minute?	*4* The downhill section?	*6* The cool down?

I gave them a moment to think about it individually before asking them to pick up a coloured cone to show me their answer (i.e. pick up a green cone if you thought it was the uphill section, a yellow cone if you thought it was the downhill section and so on).

Step two: Find someone else with the same colour cone and share your thinking.
Step three: Find someone with a different colour cone and try to persuade them you're right!
Step four: Everyone with the same colour cone was asked to group together and prepare and deliver a 30-second speech to justify their choice of colour.
Step five: Everyone could reconsider the colour of the cone they were holding.

Michael Kelly
PE teacher

Primary – reduce

The children were writing a story based on a picture for their weekly 'Big Write' activity. I displayed for the children a Lowry painting (above) and asked the children to discuss who they thought the main character was. I then asked if this painting was a story, what plot lines would there be? The children then went searching for stories within the painting.

The child to the left of the Punch and Judy stall sparked some fantastic discussions:

I think it's the child at the back because he's a piece of graffiti art.
Who has done the graffiti art?
The man in the top hat who is walking away.
Why has he drawn a boy?
Because his son was killed in an accident in a factory and he drew a picture to remind everyone of him.

I think he is floating because he is a ghost.
I think he's hanging from a nail in the wall. The man with the top hat has put him there.
Why has he done that?
Because he owns an orphanage in the city and when the children are bad, he hangs them there for everyone to see.
I think that child at the front staring at the artist is his brother. He

escaped the orphanage and he was trying to save his brother. That's why he got hung on the nail.

The stories that were developing from the painting were really thoughtful. So I then asked, *If you could give the story a title, what titles would each part have?*

'The Orphanage' was suggested, even though no orphanage is evident in the painting. The conversation had gone a long way to gathering a deeper level of thinking.

Gareth Bemister
Sidmouth CE Primary School

Reduce questions

There are a number of generic reduce questions, which can be used in a variety of situations and are particularly useful in promoting reflection and consolidation. For example, *What is the most important thing you have learned today? Which was the hardest? Which is the most important word/sentence?* are all handy questions to have up your sleeve.

However, there are also a great many opportunities to ask context-specific reduce questions, such as:

- *If Kant and Bentham were stranded on a desert island where only one can pull through, who would survive and why?*
- *Who would win in a fight – a noun or a verb?*
- *Here are two pictures of Oliver Cromwell. Which one tells you most about him?*
- *Here are three paintings. Which one is the masterpiece and why?*
- *If we had to live without one of the four main mathematical functions, which should we lose and why?*

Arguably, the key to these types of questions is the *and why?* element, and the way in which the teacher orchestrates the subsequent discussion. At this point, we would expect to hear the word *because* being used; a clear indicator that we are moving from knowing to understanding.

Thanks to Rache Stone, Rachel Hayward, Linda Hodgson, Lara Morse and Jo Hawkin for these reduce questions.

English – reduce

A strategy I have found invaluable is asking students to reduce information. I gave students a passage of information and asked them to write down the five key words – the words they thought were the most important. I then hid the passage and told students to summarise the information using only their key words as an aid. Most students were able to recall the fundamental information from the passage, and when I questioned them they had clearly developed a deeper understanding of the content through the process of reducing it. Some realised that the key words they had intially selected were in fact not the most important in the passage and these students were not as successful in summarising. When the students repeated the same exercise at a later date they were much more critical in their word choices and key elements of the passage were understood and retained. **I was amazed at how such a simple strategy – a tiny adjustment to my current practice – could have such a big impact on my students' learning.**

Gemma Gilbert
English Teacher

Following the INSET day looking at the Magenta Principles, I have noticed an immediate impact. There is definitely a heightened 'buzz' about teaching and learning and it is noticeable how many conversations are taking place about classroom practice.

There was an overwhelming feeling that the ideas made sense and because of which they were achievable for all teachers regardless of their subject area or experience. More than that, colleagues know they don't have to do more work, spend more time planning or 'reinvent the wheel' but merely tweak existing practice and resources in order to challenge students to think, to talk and ultimately develop their understanding.

John Naylor
Deputy head teacher
Brinsworth Comprehensive School

Assemble

This principle is based upon the premise that, if learning involves constructing meaning, students have to build up, or assemble, their understanding of an issue or concept. Although there are many variations, the key idea behind this approach is that, during an activity, not all of the information necessary for understanding is:

- Given in one go
- Given to any one person
- Given in the same way
- Given in completed form.

Some of the ways that students can assemble information include techniques that are well known to teachers such as **snowballing** and **jigsaw.**

Snowballing involves students working individually, then in pairs, before pairs join together to create groups. For example, *think of three possible reasons why…now join together and see if you can get five between you…* A variation on the snowballing theme – **speed dating** – can be found on page 96.

An example of a jigsaw technique can be found on page 55. In this lesson, a number of stations had been set up each containing different pieces of information relating to the execution of Thomas More. One person from each group visited the various stations before returning to their home group to share the information they had gathered.

One particularly effective version of the assemble principle is to work in small groups and distribute the information in such a way so that all students get some of it but no one person gets all of it. Only by working together and assembling information can the group make sense of it.

It can be effective to place a constraint on the activity – for example, students are allowed to tell people about the information they received but they are not allowed to show it. In other words, force them to talk!

In many respects these assemble activities are based upon and reflect much of what we know about the nature of learning:

- There is a social dimension
- Language is central
- Students are engaged in making meaning.

Maths – assemble

Working in groups of 4–6 the cards were dealt out so that each student was holding 2–3 clues. A variation – which makes the task more challenging – is to withhold the cards marked ** until a little later in the exercise.

Students are not allowed to show their clues but they are allowed to read them out. It can be helpful to issue each group with some notepaper for their workings out. **Answer is on page 216 – good luck!**

g has only got 3 factors

There are only 2 prime numbers

** There are 6 numbers to find

B is the smallest number

r is a multiple of 5

d is both an even number and a square number

All of the numbers are unique, positive integers

Half of the numbers are square numbers

r and g are both odd

All of the numbers are less than 16

a and e are both prime numbers

r and g have 2 factors in common

** If you put the letters in numerical order it makes an animal

One of the prime numbers is even

One of the prime numbers is bigger than 12

Tom Walton
The Ecclesbourne School

Primary English – assemble

This activity is based upon a 3 x 3 grid.

I used an assemble activity following on from some initial teaching about different word groups. The children had begun to understand that there were different word groups (pronouns, adjectives, articles, prepositions and so on); however, I felt that an assemble activity would provide an opportunity to develop discussion and develop and consolidate their knowledge.

I provided the children with a list of words:

am, beautiful, an, our, quickly, Manchester, over, cricket bat, consequently

We worked in groups of six and each child was given a clue. They were allowed to talk but not allowed to show the rest of the group their clue. Working together they had to place the list of words in the correct place on the 3 x 3 grid.

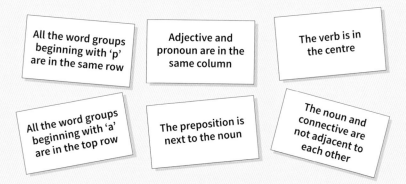

There are many variations to this exercise. For example:

- use shapes instead of words with clues such as *all of the triangles are in the same column*

- use numbers with clues such as *all of the prime numbers are in the same row* and *numbers in the corners all divide by the same number.*

Rachel Earley
Sidmouth CE Primary School

Speed dating

Speed dating is a quick and effective way to assemble – or share information.

Step one: students sit in a circle and 'number up' and then work in pairs so that 1 works with 2, 3 works with 4 and so on. The exercise begins with the odd number asking their even number partner a question. Possible questions for this exercise include *What do you know about…? What do you remember about…? What questions are you going to ask about…?* and so on.

Step two: after two minutes all of the odd numbers move one place clockwise around the group so that 1 is now partnered with 4, 3 is partnered with 6 and so on. This time the even number student asks their partner the same question. At this stage, the person answering must say, *I know…and the person I've just been listening too knew…* In other words, they add what they have just heard to what they already knew and share it with their new partner. In this way information is built up – or snowballed – during every round.

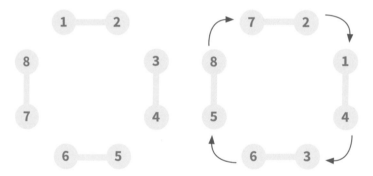

Step three: the numbers move around the group clockwise to create further new pairs. This time it's odd numbers who ask their partners the same question. Remind students to answer the question by stating both what they know/can remember and also what they have collected from their previous partners.

The process is repeated a number of times – four rounds are usually sufficient – so that each student asks and answers the question on two occasions.

An obvious time to use this technique is at the end of a lesson or unit of work, using the prompt *what can you remember?* However, it works equally well at the beginning of a topic by changing the question to *what do you know about…?*

MFL – assemble

Use the words and phrases to create as many sentences as you can.

Challenge – use the words in bold in your sentence. A variation would be to challenge students to come up with the longest and/or shortest sentence.

Suzanne McCardle
Trinity School, Carlisle

Science – assemble/change

Teaching the structure of the elbow joint is a normally mundane lesson involving diagrams, labels and descriptions. Instead, I took an existing description from a resource I had, cut it up and put the pieces in an envelope. Everyone in each small group had to piece together their information to understand the elbow joint structure and explain how it moves the arm. I asked each group to create a simple model using Play-Doh and other items of 'junk' from the prep room. Watching them attach rubber bands and Play-Doh to lollipop sticks before dismantling and reconstructing their model to incorporate the next piece of information was fascinating. I could circulate and ask higher order questions to check their understanding. The lesson flew by and they were able to demonstrate their knowledge by successfully completing an exam question. It was brilliant! Every single student was engaged and interacting, even the quiet ones, to develop an understanding. **I didn't have to create anything new; just think about how to use what I had differently (which is far more appealing to a teacher!).**

Jenny Kemp
Brinsworth Comprehensive School

Arrange

The process of arranging information, particularly when done collaboratively, is an effective way of helping students explore an issue while their final arrangement provides the teacher with a clear indication of how they are thinking.

Two of the best-known arrangement activities are:

- A diamond nine
- An archery target.

A diamond nine exercise involves students arranging information in the shape of a diamond, placing the information they believe to be the most important at the top of the diamond and the information they believe to be the least important at the bottom.

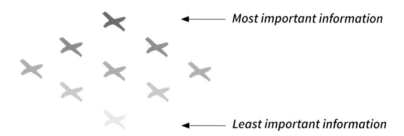

The archery target activity involves students placing the information they believe to be the most important in the centre of the target and the information they believe to be less important towards the periphery.

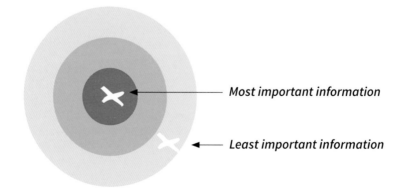

There are many variations: for example, turn a diamond nine into a diamond four; substitute the word interesting for important; give students the information to be arranged or invite them to generate their own; employ a *snowball* approach – students complete the exercise as an individual before working in pairs, small groups and finally as a whole class; ask students to physically create a diamond…

The fact that many teachers will be aware of some of the ideas in this book without being familiar with the term Magenta Principles was highlighted earlier in the book. A diamond nine is one such activity and this would be an appropriate moment at which to reinforce the point that there are a huge number of highly effective learning activities that have been developed by teachers and educationalists over many years. As has already been suggested, we did not seek to reinvent the wheel; we simply asked the question, what is the principle that underpins the strategy?

Arrange strategies are ideal activities to use with the sandwich technique outlined on page 71. For example, begin the lesson by inviting students to complete a diamond nine activity before revisiting it at the end of the lesson. Any changes that students make to their diamond are the result of how their thinking has changed and their understanding has developed during the lesson.

PE (Y9 Netball) – arrange

We were looking at defending so before the game I asked students to select the 4 positions in their team that they believed were most important to defending in the game. For example, Goalkeeper, Wing Defence, Centre and so on.

Students worked in groups of 4 and each chose a position they thought was important for defending. They physically arranged themselves in the shape of a diamond to show me their thinking; students with the most important position for defending were asked to position themselves closest to me in the diamond and the students with the least important position of defence were asked to stand further away from me. I then asked them to justify their thinking. The same task was repeated at the end of the lesson and it was surprising how many changes were made to the diamonds.

Hally Lockwood
The Brunts Academy, Mansfield

MFL – arrange

Place the most complex sentences near the middle of the target and the less complex towards the periphery. How can the sentences on the outside be made more complex and moved nearer the centre?

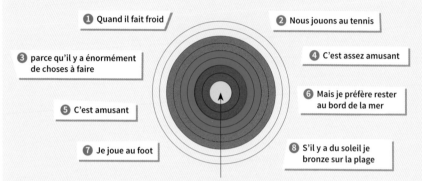

1 Quand il fait froid

2 Nous jouons au tennis

3 parce qu'il y a énormément de choses à faire

4 C'est assez amusant

6 Mais je préfère rester au bord de la mer

5 C'est amusant

7 Je joue au foot

8 S'il y a du soleil je bronze sur la plage

What could you put here? Our own choice of the best?

A great activity for promoting discussion – to say there were disagreements would be something of an understatement!

Suzanne McCardle
Trinity School, Carlisle

Geography – arrange

While they were lining up in the corridor I informed my Y8 class that the classroom they were about to enter was in fact Australia and asked them to arrange themselves in a way that accurately reflected the population distribution. Quick as a flash one boy asked, *which way is north?* – to which I replied *the side by the window.*

By the time I had entered the room, virtually all of the group were clustered together by the white board and store cupboard with a couple of children opposite at the far side of the room. I asked who they were, to which they replied, *Perth of course!*

Anthony Smith
Geography teacher

Year 6 – arrange and connect

I have used the idea of an archery target and the arrange principle with my Y6 class in a number of different ways. Both activities prompted fantastic discussion and gave me a real insight into the way the children were thinking. They also allowed me to revisit learning later on in a topic, and use a similar activity to see if their thinking and reasoning had developed further.

We have been reading *Private Peaceful* by Michael Morpurgo and so far we have been introduced to nine characters – Grandma Wolf, Colonel, Tommo, Charlie, Molly, Mother, Big Joe, Father and Mr Munnings. I asked the children to consider that if Tommo was to wake up in the middle of the night at this stage in the novel, which characters do you think would be most likely on his mind? The children had to place the character cards close to Tommo in the centre if they thought the character would be occupying his mind and further away if Tommo would not be thinking about them in the middle of the night. We revisited this activity when we had read several more chapters and considered who might be playing on his mind now, and moved our characters accordingly, also adding new ones onto the target board.

I have also used the same basic idea in a number of maths lessons. In this example students worked in pairs and were asked to arrange the numbers by placing the numbers that have a strong connection to 36 near the middle of the archery target and numbers with a weaker connection towards the outside. They were then asked to think about whether they could take 36 off and replace it with a different number that would still have similar relationships to the other numbers.

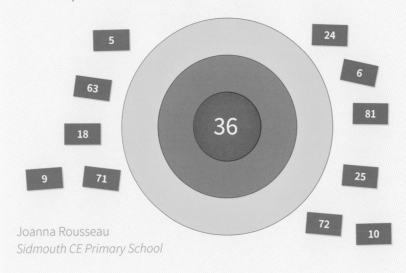

Joanna Rousseau
Sidmouth CE Primary School

Media Studies – bookends

I did this activity with a Y10 Set 5 group who are studying AQA English and AQA Media Studies. It was our first media studies lesson and I wanted them to begin to understand that colour has connotations.

Step one: The students were given a selection of cards and asked to match these cards as pairs. For example:

Step two: Students were given a set of colour cards and they had to arrange them in order ranging between their words. For example:

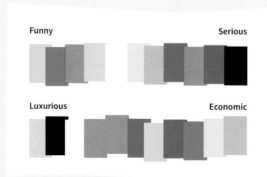

The activity provoked lots of discussion as they negotiated which colours should be placed where. For example, white and black were instantly identified with luxury, but different students had different ideas about whether black and white were sexy/innocent. We discovered that there was a distinction between how colours were viewed by different people – particularly by people of different ages – a significant point in how connotations need to be used in advertising.

Jackie Everett
Wymondham High Academy

Y12 Mechanics – reduce, arrange and connect

Students are required to draw heavily upon a number of key skills/concepts such as *using Newton's second law F = ma, adding and subtracting vectors* and *resolving a force into parallel and perpendicular components.* The idea was to give students an insight into the distribution of marks across the key concepts examined, in addition to being able to quickly identify which key concept(s) are being tested in exam questions.

Step one – reduce: Which single mechanics 1 concept will gain you the most marks in the exam? After a discussion the students agreed *resolving forces* as the most useful concept for gaining the most marks.

Step two – connect: In groups, students looked at a range of examination questions and considered which key concept would gain them the most marks when used on that particular question.

Step three – arrange: The groups then arranged the key concepts on a target; those they believed would gain them most marks were placed near the centre and those that would get them fewer marks were placed on the outside.

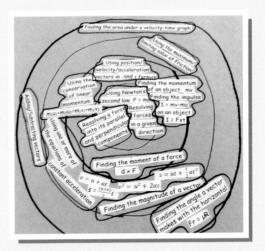

Step four – reduce: The final challenge was to complete as much of an exam paper as possible using just the two concepts considered most valuable.

The students were completely engaged and commented that not only were they now better at identifying which concept to use to solve a question but that the process had helped them to identify which concepts they still needed to work on. The greatest impact seemed to be on students working at a C/D grade who significantly improved on previous marks in a mock exam the following lesson.

Nigel Cross
Shenley Brook End School

Change

The rule of thumb is simple, whenever possible, ask students to convert the information into a different form. For example, if the students receive a diagram, ask them to describe it; if they receive text, ask them to change it to a diagram. It may be a simple strategy but **it represents a fundamental switch in emphasis, from reproducing to recreating information.** Not only do students now have to think, but the way in which they undertake the task gives the teacher a clear insight into their thought process.

To fully appreciate the significance, consider for a moment how people learn. Learning involves individuals making personal sense of information and experience. It is a meaning-making process in which new knowledge is effectively being created – or constructed – in the brain. Changing the form of information then is an approach to teaching that is firmly based upon learning.

Once again, there are many variations around the theme…

- …change text into a diagram
- turn keywords into a poem
- use anything on your desk (for example, your pencil case, homework diary and so on) to turn them into a model
- mime it
- paint a piece of music
- turn a poem into a line graph
- turn a physical movement, for example, a tennis serve, into six still frames…

…and it could come in the form of a task – in groups of four mime the way in which white blood cells attack foreign bodies – or a question – if the Duke of Ferrara was a car, which car would he be and why?

Science (Y10 Biology) – reduce and change

Students were issued with some text and first individually and then in pairs were asked to identify and underline the key words. We took some feedback from around the room to see if the same words were being selected and, if so, why.

A pathogen enters the body and is detected by a white blood cell. The white blood cell can recognise the antigens on the surface of the pathogen and moves towards it. It then changes shape to mould itself around the pathogen and then engulfs the whole pathogen. Enzymes that can digest the pathogen are then secreted to destroy it.

We then watched animations of the three different ways white blood cells attack pathogens, I split the class up into five groups of five and asked each group to concentrate on one of the ways white blood cells attack. Two groups were asked to concentrate on the same approach – this was deliberate as this particular approach is the most difficult to understand; by asking two groups to focus on it meant that it would be acted out twice to the rest of the class. This is an ideal opportunity for differentiation, with the weaker students grouped together and the brighter students challenged with the more difficult techniques. I then asked the students to act out the methods they had learned in the lesson. Each group had to have a narrator that described what was happening to the rest of the class.

This part was fantastic, with students making themselves into white blood cells and pathogens with antigens on the surface (arms sticking out). One particular group who acted out a white blood cell engulfing a pathogen and destroying it using enzymes had three students who linked arms to be the white blood cell. They then moved towards the student who was the pathogen with his arms stuck out to represent antigens on the surface. The students as the white blood cell then changed shape to 'engulf' the pathogen and then closed around in a closed circle. The pathogen student then 'sank' to the floor quickly as he was digested by the enzymes within the white blood cell.

The way the students dramatised these methods of white blood cells attacking pathogens and the detail that was included showed me that they had understood the lesson well.

Emma Clark
The Ecclesbourne School

Geography – change

I was introducing map work to a Y7 class. Half of the class received a map of Africa while the other half received a map of South America.

Step one: Working in small groups turn your map into a model (we used large sheets of sugar paper, blue wool for rivers, gravel for mountains, leaves for rainforests and so on).

Step two: Swap your model with a group that has been working on a different continent (i.e. Africa swapped with South America).

Step three: Turn your new model back into a map.

Step four: Compare your newly created map with an atlas map.

Engaging, enjoyable and memorable (only the caretaker complained about sand on the floor). However, it was much more than this. Many people have a mental block when it comes to maps and helping students understand that a map is simply a picture of a physical landscape stands them in good stead when using maps at a later stage.

Mike Hughes
Geography teacher

> **Use of Play-Doh**
> *One very simple yet very effective way of changing information is to use Play-Doh and ask the students to show their understanding in the form of a model.*

History – change

My Y10 class was studying the Truman Doctrine and Marshall Aid and I asked them to show me their understanding of the concepts in the form of a Play-Doh model.

The students explained that their model (opposite) shows General Marshall reaching out, with aid, to western Europe who are floating in the 'sea of uncertainty' being threatened by the communist sharks. This was a very imaginative concept by this particular group of four mixed-ability students who have since commented that they feel confident remembering the key concepts of both factors due to the memorable nature of the activity and that they were able to take a picture of their models to use for future revision.

I have also used the technique with my Year 12 students to help them plan an essay for the Wars of the Roses exam.

Working in groups of three the students planned an introduction that outlined their argument and then constructed three paragraphs using the Play-Doh. The idea was for students to really think about each piece of knowledge and verbally evaluate the information, which then contributed to their supported judgement in the conclusion. The class was highly engaged and enthusiastic about the activity, especially as it was memorable, which allowed them to recall their essay answers easily, both the structure and content.

I have found Play-Doh to be a highly effective tool that supports learning. Not only do students benefit from a memorable experience in the classroom, it is also an approach that helps them develop a deeper understanding of key content and/or crucial skills. Students are able to take a photo of their work and use it as an instant resource at home to support their learning further.

David Lee
Whitley Bay High School

English – change

Beloved sweetheart bastard. Not a day since then
I haven't wished him dead, Prayed for it
so hard I've dark green pebbles for eyes,
ropes on the back of my hands I could strangle with

After studying the poem *Havisham* by *Carol Ann Duffy* I asked students what feelings are shown in the poem? Most students thought that the poem was primarily about hate, apart from the word *sweetheart* in the first line. I then asked students to **turn the poem into a line graph**, plotting the love or hate shown in each line.

This was an incredibly interesting task as it encouraged the students to analyse each line and word in detail. A brilliant question it drew out from one student was *how can we plot the love or hate in this line when it is only half a sentence – the rest of the sentence is on the line before?* This allowed me to draw out the poetic technique *enjambment* and its effects. Students were able to draw out that if you look at the first and second line together it reads *Not a day since then I haven't wished him dead.* However, if you analyse only the second line it reads *I haven't wished him dead.* Two completely different meanings are therefore offered – that she has wished him dead every day, or that she has never wished him dead – highlighting the speaker's confused feelings. **I simply did not expect my year 8s to complete such higher-level analysis in an introduction to poetry.**

After completing the task I posed the same question: *what feelings are shown in the poem?* Students had to respond with evidence from the poem and the difference in response was noticeable; they had a deeper understanding of the language used but were also able to carefully select textual detail to back up their points. I also asked what was difficult about the task. A student responded saying that the language of love and hate was so mixed that it was hard for some of the lines to place it, as it was extreme love and extreme hate.

Gemma Gilbert
English teacher

Psychology – change

My Y12 Psychology group was studying bodily stress response. After initially reducing a heavy piece of text into some key words such as *Sympathomedullary Adrenal Pathway (SAM response), Hypothalmus, Adrenal Medulla* and so on – I asked them to turn what they knew into a traditional story.

The idea was that the chronology of the story should accurately reflect the order in which the body would respond to a short-term stressor, for example sudden shock or panic.

> Once upon a time in SAM land, there was a king called Hypothalmus who controlled the whole kingdom...

I think they were a little reluctant at first but they soon got into it and you could tell by their body language and the laughter that they enjoyed it. Not only was it a memorable lesson, it enabled me to check whether they'd really understood it.

One thing that stood out was how the activity benefited the less able students in particular.

Lauren Freemantle
Lutterworth College

Science – change

I challenged my group to produce a menu solely made from insects that would provide a healthy balanced diet. We would then have a class vote to select the best.

One group created a McDonald's-based meal with cockroach nuggets, ant sauce, fries and squashed caterpillar ice cream for pudding. This was voted as quite popular by the class but didn't score points for being a balanced meal. The winning meal was a caterpillar and cricket burger served with salad in the bun, which scored very highly for nutritional content.

Lyn Ottaway
Wymondham High Academy

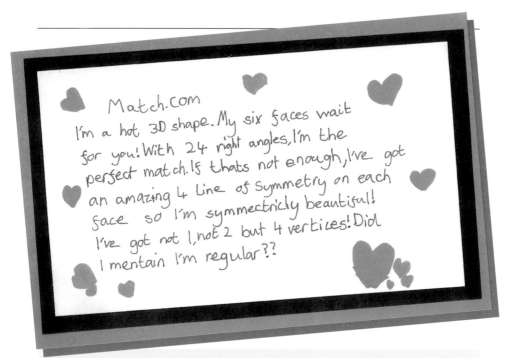

Primary maths – change

This activity came about after trying to find more interesting ways for children to use their understanding of shapes and their properties. To begin with, children discussed how they could classify shapes (number of sides, angles, dimensions, area and so on). We then created a list of criteria. I then explained the task to the children. They were to write a lonely-hearts ad for a shape of their choice, and include as many properties of the shape as possible. I gave them a few examples and after a surprisingly short time, the children understood the task and set about melting hearts with their explanations of shapes!

Gareth Bemister
Sidmouth CE Primary School

Science – change

Students worked in pairs – A's and B's

A's were issued with an information sheet, *Antibiotic Resistance – How does it happen?*, while B's were issued a different information sheet about what makes it more likely.

The layout of the sheets meant that all of the text was written on the left-hand side of the page leaving the right side blank.

Step one: Students transformed the text into pictures/visual images on the right side of the sheet.

Step two: The pages were folded in half and students had to explain the information to their partner just from the pictures.

Step three: Their partner constructed a bullet point summary of the information.

Step four: The partners swapped roles and repeated the process.

Changing the text into pictures ensured my students processed the information and developed a clear understanding of the key concepts. When listening to student conversations during the explanations, students were using key scientific terms appropriately; this is usually something that can take a whole lesson but was successfully achieved in a 15-minute activity.

Louise Bradley
Whitely Bay High School

Variety and choice

Variety and choice contribute greatly to effective teaching and learning. Children – and adults – thrive upon novelty and unpredictability, and the best teachers know that providing plenty of variety is an effective way of keeping interest levels high.

More than that, all children have a preference for different types of activity and ways of working and by mixing things up teachers have a greater chance of connecting with all children over a series of lessons. As a profession we were undoubtedly guilty of oversimplifying and exaggerating the whole issue of learning styles – children in mainstream education are not *visual* or *auditory* learners but multi-sensory learners; however, the fact that different children enjoy and respond to different ways of working is a factor that the best teachers take into account when planning activities.

The best teachers are also aware that human beings like the feeling of being in control and one of the easiest ways of doing this in the context of the classroom is to give children a choice whenever possible. For example, *we have reduced this piece of text to six key words and I would like you to turn these words into a diagram or a poem – your choice.*

There are a number of ways of doing this. For example, we could give a limited choice: *we have reduced this piece of text to the six key words and I would like you to turn them into a diagram or a poem – your choice.* Or, we could give them a completely free rein: *show me your understanding of this concept in any way you choose.* The latter approach tends to work best when students have been exposed to a wide range of Magenta Principles and the principles themselves have been made explicit.

The flexibility in the different principles is a big plus. I have a laminate on my desk at home that lists the principles and I use this as a quick reference when planning lessons. It reminds me of all the Magenta Principles available so that I can select the appropriate one depending on classes, groupings and the topics that I teach in science.

Simon Hall
Whitley Bay High School

Primary – change

One of my Y1 class – we'll call him Tom – has an auditory processing disorder and consequently struggles to retain information or instructions. During whole class activities, he will make good contributions, but when it comes to independent work he finds it difficult to produce work indicative of sound understanding. His verbal contributions when exploring descriptive writing and effective word choices are usually impressive and he often begins his work 'fired up' but after writing the first couple of words he grinds to a halt.

On one such occasion, we had worked all week towards a *Big Write*. Tom had joined in the introductory activity and had returned to his seat full of ideas. He even told me what his first sentence would be – one describing the jungle setting of his story, including squawking birds and chattering monkeys. Without having planned to do so, I suddenly decided to apply one of the ideas I had come across a few days earlier in a Magenta Principles workshop.

I asked Tom to tell me his first sentence. Then I asked him to tell me again but this time use physical gestures to accompany and represent the words. Finally, I asked him to show me the gestures without saying the words aloud.

For the first time this year, Tom was able to write down his idea in its entirety. Now and again he would pause, go through the gestures, look at me and grin, then resume writing. The difference it made to his confidence – as well as his *Big Write* that week – was amazing. It is a strategy I continue to use with success. It was such a small thing yet it made a huge difference to this particular child.

Emma Johns
Sidmouth CE Primary School

Now and again, he would pause, go through the gestures, look at me and grin, then resume writing comes from the example above and is one of my favourite lines in the entire book. Moments like these make the job worthwhile and are the reason why many teachers joined our profession. A tiny change in practice for the teacher but it made such a massive difference to the individual child.

The same technique was used by a science teacher with her Y11 GCSE class (page 51). She notes – *in years gone by students would often pick up one or two marks on this type of question but this group were picking up five or six marks. It was a noticeable improvement.*

Change / Connect Questions

These types of questions can be particularly effective at both getting students to think and getting an insight into the they way in which they are thinking. The fact that they are often a 'little bit different' appeals to many students.

Examples include:

- *How can you design a circuit so the light goes off when the switch goes on?*
- *What would have happened in the wolf had visited the brick house first? (Three little pigs)*
- *Do you think we'd all be talking German now if Hitler had invaded immediately after Dunkirk?*
- *How can you use the Pentatonic scale to create a happy mood?*
- *What would the world be like if Newton's laws didn't exist? Draw it*
- *How are plants like factories?*
- *What would have happened if the three bears had visited Goldilocks' house?*
- *If… was an animal/colour/piece of furniture/ car/punctuation mark, which would they be and why?*

Thanks to Ben Williamson, Rachel Hayward, Ellie Hughes, Lyn Ottaway and Liz Webster for these change / connect questions.

History – change/compare

For the synoptic Russia paper in A2 History the need to address seven different rulers in a single essay creates a need to succinctly identify the similarities and differences between them.

One way that I have done this is to get students to turn each ruler into a *Superhero* – each with three superpowers and three weaknesses in their 'secret identity'. For example, one student turned Lenin into *Hypnomaster* – his powers being a hypnotic gaze, hypnotic voice and hypnotic writing that allowed him to persuade people to follow his ideas. His weaknesses were that he could only hypnotise people while in Russia where he could be heard, that he depended on his friend Trotsky and that he had a bullet lodged in his neck. Tsar Alexander III, on the other hand, became *The Bear* for another student – with a bear's strength, a bear's roar to terrify people and a bear's spirit –

embodying Russia. His weaknesses were that he had a bear's temper and (because he wasn't raised to be Tsar) a bear's brain and bear's manners.

This not only opened up discussion about whether these powers and weaknesses really encapsulated the rulers, but also allowed a comparison. For example, both Lenin and Alexander III were strong rulers, but identifying their strengths and weaknesses this way helped students to see that Lenin's strength depended on his ability to get others to follow him, while Alexander's depended on his physical might and, as Tsar, the way he represented Russia.

Adam Rule
Whitley Bay High School

Art – replace

The Black Book of Colours by Menena Cottin and Rosana Faria is a book about colour for people with visual impairments. All images are embossed black on black and there is braille writing above a tiny line of white writing. The only colour in the book is black. The colours are described using all other senses.

Colours would be drawn from a hat and then the student's task would be to describe the colour without using the name of the colour but instead using all the senses. I discouraged them from relying on familiar associations: e.g. not sky is blue, or grass is green.

The variation would be to provide students with a description and invite them to work out the colour. For example, can you identify the colours being described?

Colour one:
Smells: smoky
Tastes: bitter
Sounds: muffled
Feels: cold

Colour two:
Tastes: like candy floss
Sounds: high pitched and squeaky
Smells: like clouds
Feels: like extreme heat and cold

Answers overleaf

Colour one: grey
colour two: white

The students' response to describing the colours is wary at first. Then they start to realise the weight of what I was asking them to do: help blind people see. I emphasised that they can't get it wrong: it won't or can't be checked. It's more about thinking about the emotions behind the colours, and how powerful certain colours could be if used. The really important thing is that the task encourages the students to think about art in an entirely different way.

Lara Morse
Chiltern Training Group

Primary English – replace/arrange

My Y6 group were looking at verbs. As a warm-up I challenged them to make the longest verb chain (use the last letter of a word as the first letter of the next) they could in three minutes.

For example, jum**p** – **p**inc**h** – **h**elp

I then presented them with the sentence *She looked out of the window.*

Step one: Think of as many verbs as possible that could replace the word *looked* (for example, gazed, peeked, watched, glimpsed and so on).

Step two: Think about the following scenario… *A child watching snow falling* …and arrange your list of words so that the most appropriate word for this context is at the top and the least appropriate word at the bottom (i.e. gazed would be more appropriate in this context than peeked).

Step three: Think of a scenario where the word that is bottom of your list now becomes top (they came up with things that you wouldn't want to look at for very long such as a horrible spider or a nasty injury).

Joanna Rousseau
Sidmouth CE Primary School

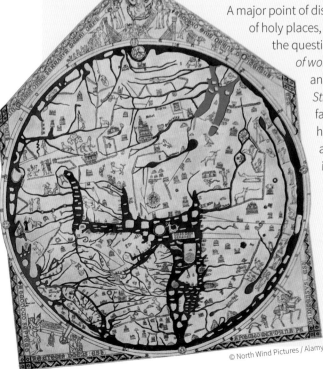
© Getty Images News / Photographer: Peter Macdiarmid

Art – compare

I asked my Y7 group what are the similarities between Grayson Perry's 2011 tapestry the *Map of Truths and Beliefs* (right) and the medieval *Mappa Mundi?* (below)

They came up with some brilliant suggestions, pointing out the similarities: both being maps of some kind, both showing holy places, places of importance, both being drawn quite crudely and naively and both not being realistic interpretations of the world or any real map. The differences they found were: Grayson Perry was more colourful and creative, the Mappa Mundi made no sense at all, the Mappa Mundi had Jerusalem at its heart as the centre of the world whereas Grayson Perry had put a gigantic eye!

A major point of discussion was Perry's choice of holy places, with one student posing the question, *why is Las Vegas a place of worship or a holy place?* and another asking, *why is Wall Street on there?* This led to a fascinating discussion about how a holy place doesn't always have to be religious in the traditional sense of the word.

Dean Sandford
Chiltern Training Group

© North Wind Pictures / Alamy

History – change

We were studying the English Civil War and I asked the students to show me the Battle of Marston Moor just by using anything that was on their desks or in their bags at the time. The photograph below shows the dictionary representing Prince Rupert's cavalry lining up behind the Royalist infantry (pencil case) and facing the Parliamentary infantry (line of pencils) across a ditch (the tie).

Ellie Hughes
History teacher

English – connect/change

Another connect strategy that I have found particularly useful and extremely engaging for the students is making a model. I have used this technique to help students develop their understanding of characters in novels and plays. I provide the students with a bag of random assorted objects from around the classroom and around the home. Students have to make a representation of the character – this might be by building a physical model, or by simply selecting objects they would associate with the character. Groups then have to explain and justify their model to the rest of the class. For example, when we were studying the playscript of *The Demon Headmaster* I gave each group a bag of objects and told them to show me their understanding of the headmaster. This was interesting as the objects were mostly feminine. One group chose a hairbrush to represent his desire for cleanliness in the world, and a lock to show he felt isolated, cut off and had no heart.

Gemma Gilbert
English teacher

English – compare

I frequently use compare questions to stimulate thought and discussion amongst my groups. I particularly like to challenge students to identify similarities between characters, items and events that are not immediately obvious.

For example, I posed the question what are the similarities between Atticus *(To Kill a Mockingbird)* and Harry Potter? The students' initial reaction was that there were none. However, before too long I began to hear comments such as, *both were thrust into difficult situations, both chose the difficult option because they believed it to be right* and *both did things they believed to be right even though it meant they might hurt the people they loved.*

It is a simple technique but it helps students explore character traits in a much greater detail.

Louise King
English teacher

ICT –change

I used the technique of reducing a piece of text and changing it – into a poem – with my Y10/11 ICT group. I have never seen a group of children so buzzing about the architecture of internal components and cache storage!

Jamie Boyer
Carlton le Willows Academy

The CPU has it's internal components
All synchronised at the right moment
Information begins to spam
As it gets stored temporarily stored in the ram
Algorithms start to subtract and plus
Then it gets distributed by the bus…

…registers are where data is stored
located in the motherboard
the CPU places the access location
for the fetch, decode and execute operation…

Geography – reduce, connect and add

I used *A river, of Course* from Mark Cowan's book *Poems for the Geography Classroom* with my mixed ability Y8 group during their work on rivers.

> ...The river soon leaves its upper confines
> And begins to meander and wander and wind.
> In places the river erodes to the side
> The channel gets bigger, deeper and wide...

Step one: the students were given a copy of the poem and asked to highlight the most important words. They were then asked to **reduce** the poem to a maximum of ten key words. The majority of the key words chosen, as intended, were actually key features that are found along the course of a river.

Step two: we then watched a short film clip about the course of a river, with students working in mixed ability pairs. One student was asked to **connect** the key words identified in the poem to the river features that appeared in the film clip while the other was asked to look out for features of the river that were shown in the film but hadn't been mentioned in the poem.

Step three: the students compared notes and were asked to identify the appropriate place in the poem the features not yet mentioned should be fitted.

Although they were focusing on the poem they were actually considering where along the course of a river each feature would be found.

Step four: finally, the pairs were challenged to **add** to the poem by creating new verses based around any of the features they had spotted on the film but hadn't been mentioned in the original poem.

This lesson was particularly effective in allowing pupils to recall the key terminology and use it confidently and precisely in following lessons to describe the course of a river in detail. The use of the poem and the video clip was a highly engaging introduction to the rivers topic that allows pupils to independently discover new terminology and use it creatively to help develop their literacy skills within this topic area.

Nikki Ashton
Geography teacher

The Magenta Principles have become an integral part of the way I plan lessons and have enabled me to create engaging and challenging activities for the classroom. There is no doubt that they have resulted in a greater emphasis on student-led activities and increased independent learning.

This approach to lesson planning has ultimately saved me time as I am able to differentiate using the same base resources (often I find creating resources the most time consuming part of planning) while still allowing students to make maximum progress. Saving time on resourcing has enabled me to spend more time on planning and developing questioning which in turn has enabled me to stretch and challenge students through a greater emphasis on higher order questioning and thinking skills.

Nikki Ashton
Geography teacher

Maths – reduce

This activity is a variation on the reduce principle and is loosely based upon the TV show *Name that Tune* that was popular a number of years ago.

Students are presented with a problem – the key is to make the problem open enough so that it can be solved in a number of different ways.

For example: $X^2 + 3X + 1 = 2X + 57$

Students then work in small groups to consider how many different ways they could solve the problem. For example, by factorising, by completing the square, by using a quadratic formula and so on.

Groups then bid against each other; *we can solve it in two ways, we can solve it in three ways* and so on. Each group then proceeds to peer teach their solution. An effective variation is to present students with a problem and challenge them to solve it in the least number of steps. Groups again bid against each other; *we can solve it in five steps, we can solve it in four steps* and so on.

Hilary Ratcliffe and Simon Mooney
Whitley Bay High School

PE – add

My Y12 AS PE Anatomy and Physiology group were studying the onset of blood lactate accumulation, or OBLA. In other words, *the point at which the concentration of lactic acid in the blood rapidly increases and where anaerobic work begins.*

The main idea is that the point at which OBLA is reached will be different for every individual, depending upon how efficient the cardiovascular and respiratory systems are and that each sport requires different levels of aerobic and anaerobic fitness depending upon exercise intensity and duration.

I gave them a graph showing the expected lactate response of a sedentary individual as exercise intensity increases (below left). Their task was to add the appropriate line on the graph for:

- A person with CHD
- Usain Bolt
- Bradley Wiggins
- An elite 400m athlete
- A triathlete

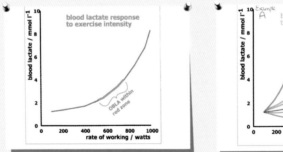 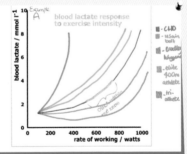

This really got the students to think as there are various factors that can affect the lactate response. The students began to talk about the topic area and how everything else can be linked into this graph and the response of different athletes. Because there are no restrictions, students can take their discussion as deeply as they wish, making this task differentiated by outcome.

Andrew Burton
Whitley Bay High School

English – add

My Y13 Literature group were studying Andrew Marvell's poem *The Garden*, which documents one person's relationship with nature. I asked the students to enlarge the poem by asking them to consider what the narrator of the poem was doing:

- Six months before
- One day before
- One day after
- Six months after

This *before, before, after, after* strategy encourages students to deepen their understanding of texts or moments in texts; allowing them to speculate on what they believe the most significant ideas in the text are.

Students responded exceptionally well to this technique and enjoyed exploring the ideas that led to the moment crystallised in the poem and the events that follow. They created wonderful back stories to explain why the narrator had retreated to the garden, mostly these centred on his inability to win 'the palm, the oak, or bays' mentioned in the poem.

I first came across the idea in a History lesson and immediately thought it would be a fabulous way of getting students to expand an idea or text. It is a technique that could easily be adapted to a number of subject areas...

Janice Burrow
Whitley Bay High School

> **Mindset**
> *Our mindset must be, if it can be done in history, what does it look like in English; if it can be done in English, what does it look like in maths...?*

Maths – add

...I first came across this idea in an English lesson and immediately thought it would be an effective technique when teaching equations. I issued my Y8 students with a flow diagram with the instruction to complete the before, before and after, after boxes (overleaf).

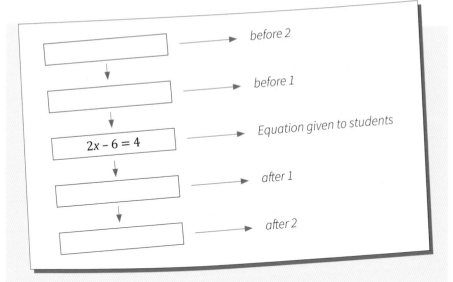

before 2

before 1

Equation given to students

$2x - 6 = 4$

after 1

after 2

The *afters* are relatively simple, as the students just need to take the equation to its natural solution. However, the *before* box involves thinking in reverse and has many possible answers. *before 2* could actually be quite tricky as you need to have an appropriate *before 1* to make it easy to manipulate into brackets.

One way of using this idea is to challenge the students to come up with as many possibilities for the *before* boxes as they can. It is a technique that encourages students to explore and manipulate equations rather than just trying to solve a specific problem. In this way they develop a much deeper understanding.

Holly Burrow
Maths teacher

The most significant feature of the Magenta Principles as far as I'm concerned is that they get students talking. A massive part of maths teaching is uncovering/avoiding/dispelling students' misconceptions and easily the most powerful way of doing this is through discussion. This can be done both as a class and as part of groupwork, where they support and challenge each other and I get to listen and gain a valuable insight into what they are thinking.

Nigel Cross
Maths teacher

Music Y1/2 – sequence

Step one: We looked at pictures of fruit and identified the number of syllables by saying the words and then clapping/counting.

123RF

Step two: We then took untuned percussion instruments and changed the word to a rhythm – different children were given pictures of different fruits (there were four different fruit types in total). The class were then 'conducted' in order to place the four fruit rhythm patterns one after another in a sequence.

Step three: The children were then put into groups of four and asked to rearrange their rhythm patterns in any order they wished, to make one long sequence – they could use their pattern as many times in succession or during the sequence as they wished. (We were actually exploring binary – AB, ternary – ABA, rondo – ABACABA…without using the subject-specific vocab at this stage….) Each group performed their piece and the children were invited to respond. Questioning was used in order to elicit from the children the recognition and understanding that the order of the sounds in the sequence when rearranged and changed made for very different compositions.

Our next sessions will allow the children to refine their pieces, exploring the musical elements of pitch, tempo, duration, dynamics and so on, building on their compositions and also creating a pictorial score.

Emma Johns
Sidmouth CE Primary School

Maths – sequence

This exercise was done with my Y12 class and was the first time they had encountered something that was solely related to AS Level rather than an extension of GCSE maths.

The focus was differentiating a function to find the equation of the tangent and I pretty much gave them some cards (below) and asked them to have a go. The idea was that students would need to consider the steps that are involved and the order in which the cards need to go.

The exercise certainly opened up a huge amount of dialogue and there were lots of conversations about what was important and what went where. It was interesting and insightful to listen to them thinking aloud in this way. Initially, they worked in pairs before we came together as a whole class with the challenge of placing the cards in the correct order.

There are a number of variations to this activity. For example:

- Leave a couple of cards blank for the students to complete
- Challenge the students to identify any cards/steps that are not necessary
- Ask the students to identify any additional steps/cards that would help someone who is struggling

Sukhi Sarai
Lutterworth College

$y = 8 - 3x^{\frac{1}{2}}$

$\dfrac{dy}{dx} = -\dfrac{3}{2}x^{\frac{1}{2}}$

$f(x) = -\dfrac{3}{2} \times \dfrac{1}{\sqrt{x}}$

$f(4) = -\dfrac{3}{4}$

$y = 2$

$f(4) = -\dfrac{3}{2} \times \dfrac{1}{\sqrt{4}}$

Gradient of the Normal $= \dfrac{4}{3}$

$y = 8 - 3\sqrt{4}$

$y - y_1 = m(x - x_1)$

$y - 2 = \dfrac{4}{3}(x - 4)$

$3y - 6 = 4(x - 4)$

$3y - 6 = 4x - 16$

$3y - 4x + 10 = 0$

Find the equation of the normal to the curve $y = 8 - 3\sqrt{x}$ at the point where $x = 4$

$y = 8 - 3\sqrt{x}$

English – reduce, connect, sequence

We are studying *Tess of the D'Urbervilles*. We have covered the first three phases so far and have been focusing upon the landscapes that Hardy presents Tess working in and travelling through.

Students were presented with three images

123RF

iStock

123RF

Step one – reduce: Which image is most representative of Tess and the function of her journeys?

Step two – sequence: Place the images in the order which best represents the changing nature of Tess and the journeys she undertakes.

Step three – connect: Which image best represents her view of herself? Society's view of her?

The questions based upon the images generated some extremely sophisticated discussion with the students commenting upon how the abstract nature of the images had really made them think deeply in order to connect image to text.

For example, one student felt that Tess' perspective was best represented by the lake landscape while society's view was the train. He concluded that Hardy's message was that it is actually impossible for these views to be reconciled and that is the tragedy of the tale. Society – as represented by the power of the train – could not be changed from its course.

Fiona Hepton
Whitley Bay High School

Maths – sequence

Step one: Students are given a set of cards with statements such as:

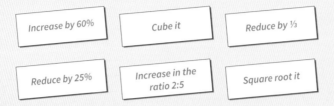

Increase by 60%

Cube it

Reduce by ⅓

Reduce by 25%

Increase in the ratio 2:5

Square root it

Step two: Students are given a starting number, for example 77.

They then have to sequence the cards so that they get the highest possible total after doing each operation in the correct order.

There are many variations to this activity, for example achieve the lowest number or arrive at a specified target number. The task can be differentiated through both the number of cards and the nature of the operations. Students could also be given the opportunity to take a card away or if groups have different cards they could trade one. Another variation is to challenge students to make up a set of cards for other groups to use.

I have used versions of this task across the ability and age range and it works especially well as a starting activity, even more so when students are able to write on the tables when trying out their different orders. The subsequent discussion about the reasoning behind their choices can lead to real insights into their conceptual understanding of concepts such as percentages, for example, *I put the reduce by 25% first so that I am reducing the least amount.*

Nigel Cross
Shenley Brook End School

What I like best about the Magenta Principles is how simply and straightforwardly they can be integrated into lesson planning and yet how much payback you get in terms of understanding: the benefits to students are really noticeable.

Louise Bradley
Biology teacher, Whitley Bay High School

Supper at Emmaus by Caravaggio, 1601 © FineArt/Alamy

Art – sequence

We were studying *The Supper at Emmaus* (above). It is a painting by Caravaggio that shows the resurrected Jesus revealing himself to two of his disciples. However, for anyone who does not know the painting, it is not immediately apparent that it is Jesus, not least as he is depicted beardless. In all, there are four people in the painting; three are seated around a table of food and a fourth man is shown standing.

I wanted them to start thinking deeply about the painting, so I asked them in which order did the characters enter the room. It is not the kind of question that I would normally ask about a painting and I was amazed at the depth of their replies and they way in which the discussion unfolded.

Rebecca Cooper
Art teacher

Connect

Making connections and placing things into a wider context are central to developing a deeper understanding. In simple terms, it is how we learn – by connecting new and existing information and by incorporating what is new to us into our existing knowledge.

In many respects making connections is the key to moving from knowing – seeing solitary pieces of information in isolation – to understanding – seeing how they relate to one another. Any teaching strategy that makes these connections explicit and helps students see the wider context, for example **snap, information dominoes, pairs** and **odd-one-out,** is helpful. They are much more than light-hearted games; they are valid and worthwhile learning activities based upon a clear rationale.

Information dominoes and snap are played just like the traditional games. Students are issued with cards that contain information: for example, numbers, shapes, words, fictional characters, elements and so on. The rule is that students are allowed to lay their card – in dominoes – or call *snap* if they can make a valid connection between the information on the card they are about to lay and the information on the card that has just been laid. Other students in the group are allowed to challenge bogus connections.

Classify

Connect comes in various guises and there are a number of approaches that are often referred to as discrete Magenta Principles that are actually underpinned by the ability to make connections. For example, classifying information is an activity frequently employed in both primary and secondary classrooms, yet the ability to group information – words, numbers, images, characters and so on – is dependent upon the ability to make valid connections.

Of course, the label doesn't matter; the fact that we are challenging students to think does.

Metaphor

You cannot create a metaphor without first making a connection and, given the significance of making connections in the learning process, metaphors are not surprisingly frequently heard in the classroom. However, it is the teacher who often provides the metaphor – or, in other words, gives students the connection. Instead, invite the students to create the metaphor and rather than receiving the connection they are required to make their own.

Primary – information dominoes

I use *information dominoes* across all areas of the curriculum, from connecting key words in Geography, to characters in English and even to famous paintings in art.

In Y2 maths the children had been learning about 2d and 3d shapes and their properties and I used this activity at the end of lesson to consolidate learning and maths vocabulary and also to give an opportunity for new learning. The class had a very wide range of ability, including some children on P scales, and so in order to involve everyone I gave just one 2d shape card to those less able children and a greater number of cards with more complex shapes on them, including 3d shapes they hadn't encountered before, to the more able members of the class.

I explained to the children that we were going to play connection dominoes and gave a brief explanation of how the game worked – they could place their card if they could tell me something that linked their shape to any others on the board.

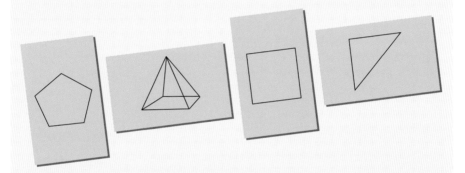

For example, one child connected a square to a triangle because they were 2d shapes; another also connected a square to a triangle but because they both contained a right angle; while another more able child could connect a pentagon to a square based pyramid because one had 5 sides and one had 5 vertices.

All the children were involved and they loved this game. It enabled me to hear their understanding of the properties of shape and their maths vocab and also to draw out more understanding by asking them if they could think of another way of connecting the shapes.

Rachel Hayward
Y2/3 Teacher

MFL – connect

I played my Y8 group who are studying German the traditional Icelandic folk song *Krummavísur* (in Icelandic!). The idea was to demonstrate to students that by reducing text it is often possible to work out the gist, even when the majority of the words are unfamiliar.

The students were issued with the Icelandic lyrics arranged line by line and another set of cards with the English translations (below). By looking for clues – similarities between the languages in terms of cognates, capital letters, punctuation, position of words within a sentence and so on – the students had to match the Icelandic and English lyrics.

We then applied these new skills to the language they were learning – German – by looking at a piece of text at a level far higher than the one they were currently working at and trying to work out the meaning without knowing all of the words.

This activity really highlighted the skills that learners need to become competent linguists and students were incredibly enthusiastic about the activity itself. Perhaps most importantly, it was amazing to see the confidence that this activity instilled in the students to tackle unknown texts – knowing that there are always techniques that can be used and understanding that 'educated guesses' are an integral part of learning have made this class more willing to take risks and ultimately achieve more in their German lessons.

Sara DelGaudio
The Ecclesbourne School

Answers on page 216

nóttu	If I go to a house
undan stórum steini	forbids me
ef að húsum heim	You can't get anything at the beach
Allt er frosið	What can a raven eat?
bannar mér	night
ekkert fæst við ströndu mor	Everything is frozen
dagur	Underneath a big rock
hvað á hrafn að éta?	day

Maths – connect

This activity is based upon the well-know card game *pairs*. I display a number of cards on the board and students 'turn them over' two at a time. I then tell them if there cards are a pair or not but do not tell them why.

For example, if we were using the cards above and the students turned over 1 and 0.1 I would say no. However, if they turned over 1 and –1 I would say yes. Gradually, they are able to work out that the connection, on this occasion, is perpendicular gradients. A variation is to allow the students to keep the pair if they can make a valid connection between the two cards.

Tom Walton
The Ecclesbourne School

Primary – connect

I really liked the idea of playing pairs and decided to adapt the principle to my Y3 class. It was relatively easy to do this in maths and a good way to get the children thinking about number bonds. I then decided to try the same idea out using words. During our *Guided reading* sessions we had been looking at various word groups so I gave the children a selection of cards with words such as *running, happily, because, cooking, and, bee, Sarah, reading* and so on. If the children turned over running and happily I would say no – without telling them why. If, however, they turned over running and cooking I would say yes; the connection being they are both verbs. The activity gave them the opportunity to put into practice what they had leant about verbs, nouns, adverbs, adjectives and connectives. They had to think really hard the first time we played but on subsequent occasions have found the connections much easier to make.

Rachel Hayward
Y2/3 teacher

Science – connect

In year 13, biology students had been taught how insulin is released from the pancreas tissue in response to increased glucose levels; they had also been taught a few months earlier how neurotransmitters are released from the end of nerve cells. I asked them to compare the processes and find similarities and differences. The list that was generated was great and there were lots of *ooo, don't they both do this...?* noises around the room and an obvious excitement that the body is very complex but actually relies on similar mechanisms for both processes.

A few months later in a new module, I picked up a board pen and asked the class *how does my brain tell the muscle in my arm to contract?* I suggested that they already knew the answer, or could work it out. To give them a nudge in the right direction I showed them their whiteboard work from three months earlier and gave them one clue; calcium is needed to bind to something in the muscle to allow it to contract.

They looked over it and then started having real conversations. Some groups started from the end point of calcium, so thought it might involve voltage gated channels; other groups started off with neurones and sodium channels and depolarisation. By the end of the activity they had used prior learning to solve most of the problem and, by exploring similarities and differences, had effectively reduced the body's seemingly complicated processes into a series of steps.

I think the reason why this activity was so useful was that it gave the students a far deeper understanding of how the body functions that wouldn't have been possible had they learnt the material in a traditional teacher taught approach. Just before they left for their examinations I gave them an essay for revision purposes with the title *With reference to the year 13 course material – what is the role of calcium in the body?* It was clear from reading their work that their retention of these detailed processes was far greater than a previous year's class, when I had taught the modules as separate entities ready for modular exams.

Lyn Ottaway
Wymondham High Academy

English Y12 – connect

I wanted to introduce my new Y12 group to the six methods that are used to analyse texts – it is crucial that they fully grasp these methods because they will rely heavily upon them throughout the course.

To begin with I asked them to research the six terms *graphology, phonology, grammar, discourse, lexis and pragmatics* independently. Rather predictably, when I questioned them they could all trot out the Wikipedia definition but when given some text and asked to pull out the pragmatics they struggled.

In order to get them thinking more deeply I asked them to allocate each of the six methods to a room or aspect of a house. For example, one group suggested that pragmatics – the implied meaning of the text – would be the window because by looking through the window you are able to see what is inside. Another group likened pragmatics to the furniture because it is the furniture that sets the tone and defines how a house feels.

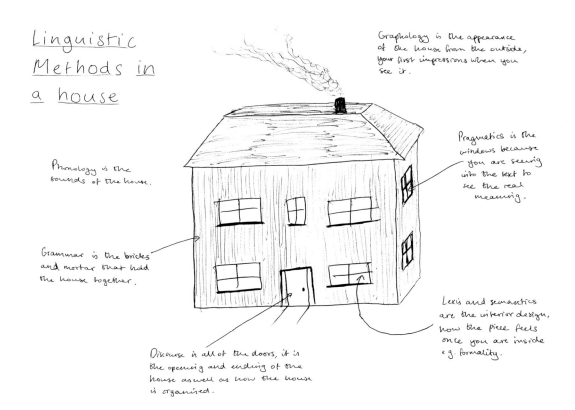

Linguistic Methods in a house

Graphology is the appearance of the house from the outside, your first impressions when you see it.

Phonology is the sounds of the house.

Pragmatics is the windows because you are seeing into the text to see the real meaning.

Grammar is the bricks and mortar that hold the house together.

Lexis and semantics are the interior design, how the piece feels once you are inside e.g. formality.

Discourse is all of the doors, it is the opening and ending of the house as well as how the house is organised.

Having completed the house metaphor I asked them to rewrite their definitions of the six methods. They had originally defined pragmatics as *the way in which context contributes to meaning and the effect on the audience* – technically correct but they didn't have a clue what it meant! They now defined it as the *hidden meaning and reading between the lines.* Now it made sense!

Katie Spurr
St Thomas More School, Blaydon-Upon-Tyne

Maths – connect

There are many variations but the basic idea is to use images of famous buildings to get students thinking about straight line graphs. This activity works equally well as either an introduction or a recap. It can also be adapted and used with very able students looking at quadratic/cubic/reciprocal and trigonometry graphs using pictures of buildings with curved sides. The activity is ideally suited to the use of graph drawing software packages that allow students to experiment and then adapt their graphs quickly and efficiently.

123RF

Step one: Issue students with images of buildings (with or without axes superimposed) and ask them to place them into two piles (specify according to their mathematical properties if necessary). The task naturally prompts discussion about the properties of the buildings and the lines needed to draw them. If needed, **y = mx + c** or similar could be put on the board as a hint.

Step two: At this point the strategies for drawing straight line graphs will need to be covered/reinforced in a manner and depth appropriate to the particular class.

Step three: Issue students with a new image (the discussions and subsequent teaching should give a really good idea of the level of understanding of each group so they can now be handed a picture that will challenge them). Their task is to write the instructions that someone else could use to draw the outline of your building using equations of straight lines. Also inform the class that they will need to limit the values, i.e. y = 4x + 1 for x between 3 and 7.

Step four: Groups swap instructions and are challenged to draw an outline of the building and guess what it is.

....

For example, using the following equations with suitable limits:

Equation 1	$y = 1.5x + 1$	*Equation 4*	$y = 1 - 0.25x$
Equation 2	$y = 8 - 2x$	*Equation 5*	$y = x - 4$
Equation 3	$y = 5 - 0.5x$		

produces a pyramid

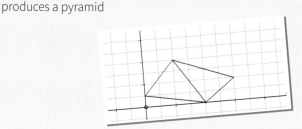

Can you guess what building the following equations (with suitable limits) make?

Equation 1	$y = x^2$	*Equation 4*	$y = 2$
Equation 2	$y = (x - 5)^2$	*Equation 5*	$y = 1$
Equation 3	$y = 4$	*Equation 6*	$y = 3$

Answer overleaf

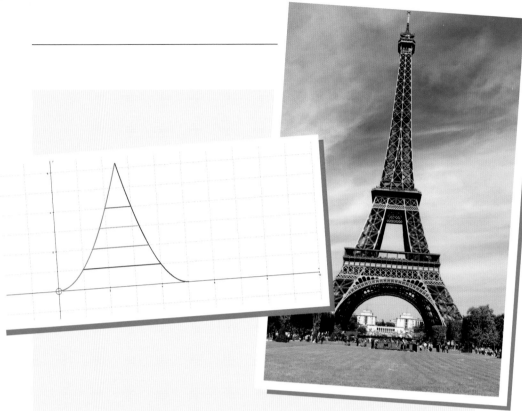

123RF

This activity is hugely successful, prompting discussion and getting students thinking. As with many similar activities, it is heavily dependent upon teacher intervention and judgement regarding the class's ability to draw straight lines and then to map them to pictures.

The original idea for this activity came from a non-mathematician and was further developed by Nigel Cross and Tom Walton.

The maths example above was not planned by a mathematician but by a PE teacher. Creating opportunities for teachers to work in pairs and small groups and for non-specialists to plan lessons can be a hugely effective professional development experience for a number of reasons: first, we challenge the mindset of *my job is to teach maths* and switch the emphasis to helping children learn; second, we emphasise the idea of principles not strategies, a philosophy that underpins the entire Magenta Principles approach; and third, we encourage teachers to look at things with fresh eyes from a different perspective.

Mathematicians think like mathematicians; linguists think like linguists. Sometimes we need a completely different mindset to provide the spark that will enable us to develop our practice.

Primary art – classify

I wanted my Y3 class to learn about the Brazilian artist Romero Britto during our World Cup topic in order for them to create their own Britto inspired art. Instead of creating a PowerPoint telling them about Britto's paintings I wanted them to pick out the key elements of his work.

I gave pairs of children a selection of about 12 pictures of works of art by Romero Britto and a variety of other artists. I didn't give them any instructions apart from to sort the pictures into two piles. Romero Britto's work is very colourful and I anticipated that they would sort the pictures very simply into bright colours and dull colours; however, what I heard as I walked around the class was amazing, with children sorting them into modern and old fashioned, fun and boring, child-like and grown up and so on.

After a while I stopped them and we shared a few of their ideas, and then I asked the children to sort the pictures into three piles. This meant they had to look much more carefully at the pictures in order to pick out a way to classify them. They were slower to get going but in listening to ideas from others on their tables they were able to complete the task.

Finally, I brought them together as a class and we sorted them on the white board. They had almost all separated the Romero Britto pictures into one group. At this point I explained about Romero Britto and his connection to our topic. I told them that we were going to create our own pictures using his style and that I wanted them to pick out some key features of his work that we could use as guidelines when making our own works of art.

The lesson was far more successful than simply showing the children a PowerPoint as all the children were fully involved. They had to think about the pictures and verbalise their thinking. Weeks down the line they could recall key features. As a bonus, the lesson was also fantastic for extending their vocabulary.

Rachel Hayward
Y2/3 teacher

English – connect

Future quotes is an activity that I have used with many different books with great success. The basic idea is that, when studying a novel or a play and we are far enough into the story to have been introduced to the main characters, students are presented with a range of quotes from later in the book and challenged to identify who said it. It is an activity that always kick-starts brilliant discussion and helps students develop a much deeper understanding of both character and plot.

On this occasion my Y10 group was working towards an essay on character change on either *Macbeth* or *Lady Macbeth*. We had read about half of the play, and had created character profiles for the two characters. The class was set in their views: Lady Macbeth was the evil manipulator, and Macbeth, a loyal soldier who had fallen victim to his own ambition. I used the future quotes activity to challenge their current perceptions, hoping it would encourage in-depth language analysis and would also serve to demonstrate how Shakespeare progresses the two characters. What was particularly effective about this activity was that students started thinking a lot deeper about character traits, tone of voice and prior knowledge. Some analysed the language until they had teased out the right answer, and each quote sparked a lively debate.

Macbeth or Lady Macbeth? Fully explain your answer. Consider prior knowledge, themes, context and language analysis.

I have no spur to prick the sides of my intent (but only vaulting ambition, which o'erleaps itself and falls on the other).	The thane of Fife had a wife. Where is she now? – What, will these hands ne'er be clean?	Here's the smell of the blood still. All the perfumes of Arabia will not sweeten this little hand. Oh, oh, oh!
Explanation	Explanation	Explanation

I gave students the first half of quote 1, feeling the word *ambition* would immediately lead students to choose Macbeth. The class was divided in opinion, with some arguing that Lady Macbeth had been full of *intent* from the offset, and others arguing that it was reference to Macbeth's ambition. However, the deciding factor came down to the self-reflective nature of the comment. One student pointed out that Lady Macbeth was determined in her desires, and was not reflective and remorseful. This led to the correct conclusion that the line was spoken by Macbeth, who repeatedly acknowledges his misguided ambition, but lets it get the better of him.

The second two quotes led to more controversy. Both lines show guilt and remorse, character traits that students did not currently attribute to Lady Macbeth. One student argued that quote 2 is spoken by Macbeth, expressing his guilt at having murdered Macduff's family. This is backed up, another student said, by the reference to his hands, as he was also shocked by the blood on his hands after murdering Duncan. Students were connecting events and using prior knowledge in impressive detail.

Gemma Gilbert
English teacher

Maths – classify

Students are issued with approximately 25 cards each containing information – for example, numbers, shapes and so on. Working in pairs, students are asked to categorise the information and divide the cards into two piles. They can do this in any way providing they can justify their thinking.

The students then repeat the process but this time divide the cards into three piles. It can be helpful at this stage to move the students about and join pairs together to form groups. Finally, the groups must discuss, justify and agree how to split the cards into four piles and explain why – this is the hardest step.

This technique helps students make new connections, forces them to consider topics in a more out-of-context setting and sets them up nicely to start a new body of work with their minds already along the right tracks.

Simon Mooney
Whitley Bay High School

English – change/connect

We have been studying the poem *My Last Duchess* by Robert Browning. I asked my mixed-gender group, *If the Duke were chocolate, broccoli or spaghetti, which would he be and why?* However, to my all-boy set, I posed the question, **If the Duke of Ferrara was a car, which car would he be and why?**

Teacher: OK, Michael, what do you think?

Michael: I thought a BMW M3 because in the poem it talks about him being commanding and powerful and the M3 has got a powerful engine.

Teacher: And how in the poem does he express how powerful he is?

Michael: Through the poem how he kills the Duchess using his power.

Teacher: Can you define that? He never explicitly says he kills her.

Michael: Somewhere in the poem it says about how he gave the command and all was quiet and that's a reference to him telling someone to kill her.

Teacher: And where else in the poem do we get the idea that he is powerful particularly, and where he might show physical power?

Pause…

Michael: At the end it says he got a bronze carving of him taming a sea horse.

Teacher: So Neptune taming a sea horse – so that's a metaphor for his power.

Teacher: Joel, what do you think about the lorry idea?

Joel: The lorry's like the biggest and most intimidating thing on the road and that's the same as the Duke in the poem – the servants are like the forecourt, which keeps the Duke going and then the Duchess is like the load the lorry's carrying and the lorry's completely in control and dictates the destiny.

Teacher: I like the idea that he is driving her to a destination, and what destination is he driving her to?

Joel: Death.

Teacher: An implied death – really good answer.

Michelle Thresher
Lutterworth College

Much the same smile? This grew; I gave commands;
Then all smiles stopped together. There she stands
As if alive. Will't please you rise? We'll meet
The company below, then…

My Last Duchess by Robert Browning

Primary – change/connect

The idea for this lesson came from Walt Disney's *Robin Hood*. The film is a cartoon and animals are used to portray the characters – the idea being that the character of the animal reflects the character of the person. For example, Robin Hood is a wily fox. I decided to try it first on a small scale during our morning warm-up activity. My Y3 class know that Monday is *Big Question* day, when I post a new big question on the white board and they have an opportunity to come up with an answer – invariably there is no right answer – and also to post their own big questions from which I choose the best one every week to pin on the big question display board. The children love it and look forward to it every week. I also pin a copy on my classroom door for passers-by to see.

The question I asked on this occasion was, **If Cinderella was an animal what would she be and why?** There were some fairly predictable answers making the connection between her sweet nature and cute animals like rabbits; however, later that day one particularly thoughtful little boy came up to me enthusiastically and said, *I've been thinking about our big question and I have a good answer. I think she would be a badger because during the day badgers hide away underground, just like Cinderella trapped in the cellar doing all the jobs for the ugly sisters, but at night they come out and play, and that's like Cinderella because it's night time when she goes to the ball and is finally free to be herself and have fun.*

This idea takes no time at all to prepare but gives a welcome opportunity for creative thinking.

Rachel Hayward
Y2/3 teacher

For me the most significant feature of the Magenta Principles has been connect. Making connections between a series of skills, key ideas or interpretations has ultimately led to a deeper understanding of an issue or critical concept of literature, which has resulted in students more easily accessing the higher mark grade criteria. There have been more 'light bulb moments' as a consequence and greater engagement.

Michelle Thresher
Lutterworth College

Geography – reduce/change

The first time that I consciously used the Magenta Principles was in the *Onion Skin Weathering* lesson briefly described on page 23; it is a lesson that I have recounted many times since and an exercise that I frequently use during Magenta Principle workshops. It seems appropriate to end this section with this example.

Onion skin weathering takes place in deserts and is the result of rock being heated and cooled over a long period of time. During the heat of the day the outer layer of the rock expands slightly and as the temperature falls at night the rock contracts. Continual expansion and contraction gradually weakens the rock until eventually bits of rock peel off – like layers of an onion.

A Y8 class were presented with the paragraph (above) and, working individually at first, asked to highlight the six key words. We used a simple snowball technique and continued the process in pairs and then small groups before a student was selected to suggest the six key words.

These were written on the board:

Heated	Contract
Cooled	Peel
Expands	Onion

I responded by asking which of the *W questions* displayed around the room (what, why, where, when and so on) couldn't be answered from the list of words on the board. A number of students virtually simultaneously answered *where* and went on to suggest that *desert* should be added to the key word list. I pointed out that we now had seven key words but were only allowed six…

The discussions continued and in total around 10 words were put forward as possible key words. My role was to orchestrate and manage the discussion, playing devil's advocate, asking for justification and so on.

There is no doubt that the seemingly simple task of reducing text had generated a good deal of thinking and discussion and it was very obvious to me from their contributions the depth to which individual students grasped the concept.

There is equally no doubt, however, that while the simple task of reducing text was the catalyst and would inevitably result in some learning taking place, the onus was very much on me as the teacher to draw out the learning and fully exploit the potential of the activity.

Having discussed how the text could be reduced to six key words I then asked the students to work in groups and gave them a few minutes to prepare a mime to demonstrate the process of onion skin weathering. While they were doing so I circulated the room, listening and observing; intervening only when necessary.

The first mime consisted of a group of children arm in arm moving together and apart in an exaggerated fashion to illustrate the way in which the rock expands and contracts. It was a bit like watching people doing the hokey-cokey! One by one students peeled away from the group – some of them in a most dramatic fashion.

I asked the group to perform their mime a second time, but before they did I asked the rest of the class to read the second sentence of the original paragraph and identify the two key words. As the mime was performed for a second time I read aloud the second sentence emphasising the words *outer* and *slightly*. As I did so the penny dropped for a great many of the group. The point that I was trying to make was that while the original mime was a decent representation of the onion skin weathering I wanted to explore the process in a little more depth.

I then asked all the groups to improve their performances concentrating upon accuracy and attention to detail rather than producing a piece of drama for dramatic effect. While they were doing so I talked to some of the more able students about why it was only the outer layer that expanded, the conductivity of rock and so on.

Two things are worth highlighting from this example:

- The lesson was memorable and enjoyable. However, it was far more than simply a bit of fun. Students understood the process because they had engaged with it.

- They key role played by the teacher. The principles of *reduce* and *change* are just the catalyst; the onus is upon the teacher to facilitate and draw out the learning.

Playing snap could be little more than a game or gimmick; however, helping students make connections could be an integral part of a rich and worthwhile learning experience. The difference between the two is not the activity but interpretation and implementation, and the support, guidance and intervention of the teacher.

Not ready-meals

The warning has already been issued on page 41 but it is important to repeat it here – the Magenta Principles are not ready-meals. To mix metaphors, think of a tent; the fabric is ineffective without the structure provided by the poles. So too the Magenta Principle activities; they are of limited value without the support and mediation of the teacher. Playing snap *could* be little more than a game or gimmick; however, helping students make connections *could* be an integral part of a rich and worthwhile learning experience. The difference between the two is not the activity but interpretation and implementation, and the support, guidance and intervention of the teacher.

In particular, two dimensions – the tent poles – are central to the Magenta Principles approach:

- Facilitation
- Consolidation.

Although they have been separated in this section for ease of understanding, facilitation and consolidation are interwoven. Consolidation is actually an integral component of the wider process of facilitation – a small Russian doll inside a larger Russian doll.

Facilitation

The task is only one element of a complex learning process. Learning occurs when individuals talk, think and engage with experiences and activities; a well-designed task therefore is important as it increases the chances that children will be engaged but it does not guarantee that learning will take place.

The extent to which the potential of the activity is exploited is largely dependent upon the way teachers manage and mediate the experience. The best teachers observe, listen, probe and intervene, and through skilful questioning and timely interventions are able to extend thinking and deepen understanding. It is the reason why exactly the same task employed by two different teachers will lead to learning experiences of varying depth and quality. The task is the constant; the variable, arguably the key variable, is the facilitation.

The teaching spectrum

INSTRUCTION   FACILITATION

Giving students   Helping students
the picture   join the dots

The best teachers are comfortable and competent at both
ends of the spectrum. They are able to judge where they
need to be on any given occasion, sensing when to tell and
when to ask, when to speak and when to listen, when to
intervene and when to leave well alone.

It is easy to nod in agreement at this point. Facilitation is one of those words that is heard frequently in the world of education; it raises no eyebrows, it slips easily off the tongue and is undoubtedly a good word to use at an interview. However, it is highly debatable whether everyone who uses it fully understands what it actually means. Yet, understanding is a prerequisite; for facilitation is as complex and challenging as it is crucial. Put simply, it is highly unlikely that a teacher is going to be a highly skilled facilitator if they are unsure what the role truly entails.

For now, let us think of teaching as a spectrum ranging from instruction at one end to facilitation at the other. **Instruction entails providing students with the complete picture, whereas facilitation involves helping individuals join the dots.**

From the outset let us acknowledge that both instruction and facilitation have a role to play. The best teachers understand this and are comfortable and competent at both ends of the spectrum. They are able to judge where they need to be on any given occasion, sensing when to tell and when to ask, when to speak and when to listen, when to intervene and when to leave well alone.

We need to dispel any myth that teachers shouldn't talk and that children need to find out everything for themselves. High quality exposition is still the hallmark of a good teacher, for when done well it can make a significant contribution to a child's understanding. The key is to be in instructor mode when appropriate and for the right reasons, not simply because it is easier and quicker. Instruction has a place; however, we must be aware that it can be a limited and limiting approach – particularly if overdone.

The verb *sensing* was deliberately used a little earlier, and the question remains the extent to which facilitation is an intuitive, instinctive thing – a gift that the best teachers are born with. Maybe there is an intuitive dimension but a large element of facilitation involves learnable skills. The verb *judge* was also used, again quite deliberately, as high quality facilitation is based upon, and is the result of, decision-making. While the decision-making may oscillate between a conscious and a subconscious process, it is decision-making nonetheless.

Part of the learning process involves moving from a state that is often referred to as *conscious competence to unconscious competence.* In other words, when we are developing a new expertise we have to think about it before we are eventually able to operate without conscious thought. Many of the Professional Development tools and experiences outlined in this section of the book involve encouraging teachers to think at a conscious level in order that they may operate more effectively at a sub-conscious level as a result.

Facilitation involves making a series of decisions **before**, **during** and **after** the experience.

Before: providing the dots

During: helping students join them

After: helping students reflect upon the picture they have created

Before we examine the decision-making process in a little more detail, let us remember the wise words of Reuven Feuerstein and his helpful rule of thumb that teachers should *mediate as little as possible but as much as necessary*.

If we compare this ideal with typical classroom practice, it is apparent that many teachers and support staff intervene too much too quickly, and when they do so *intervention* becomes *interference* – the difference being that one is helpful.

Conversely, many people mistakenly take facilitation to mean the teacher *not doing anything* or *letting them get on with it*. It may, of course, be appropriate to do nothing – but that needs to be the result of a conscious decision and because the teacher judges that intervention is not necessary at this point. In this respect, the teacher is doing something – they are not interfering.

One of the many challenges facing teachers is the sheer pace at which these decisions have to be made – classrooms are frenetic places. Teachers need to think, yet teachers get precious little time to think. This is why video is such a potentially powerful and effective tool for professional development – it has a pause button! In a similar way, the following structure – based upon the join the dots metaphor – can help teachers think things through in advance of a lesson and provide a support mechanism to fall back on in the hurly-burly of the classroom.

Before, during and after

Facilitation involves making a series of decisions before, during and after the experience.

> *Before....... providing the dots*
> *During ...... helping students join them*
> *After .... helping students reflect upon the picture they have created*

Before – providing the dots
- What do I want students to achieve from this experience?
- Where should I be on the instructor–facilitator spectrum in order to achieve this?
- What kind of dots do these particular students need?
- Do any individual students need more/fewer dots?
- How far apart should they be placed?

The intervention cycle

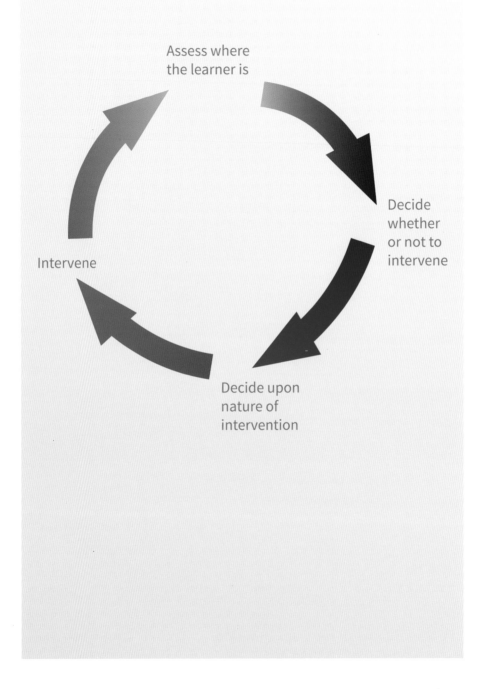

Assess where the learner is

Decide whether or not to intervene

Decide upon nature of intervention

Intervene

During – joining the dots

The before stage involves providing the dots and can therefore be planned in advance. The during bit, however, cannot be planned in the same way as it is totally dependent upon the way students respond to tasks, activities and information. In many respects it is a response to a response. It is a decision-making process that can be broken down into three key steps.

Step one: assess where the learner is

This step involves getting a clear picture about exactly what is going on in the mind of individual students. A number of points are worth highlighting:

- Teachers cannot assess understanding if the task does not allow the students to demonstrate it. There are implications here for step one.
- Teachers must observe and, in particular, listen very carefully to establish a picture of how the student is thinking.
- Listening in many respects holds the key. Quite simply, it is easier to assess a child's understanding by listening to them rather than by talking at them.
- There is a double benefit here, for if you are listening and *assessing* understanding, they must be talking – and talking helps them *develop* understanding.
- Pauses and periods of silence are integral to facilitation. In most interactions between people there is very little gap between one person finishing talking and the other starting. Indeed, often there is an overlap! When facilitating it can be extremely beneficial to pause after the student has finished talking – just a split second longer than is either normal or comfortable. Silences are awkward and are consequently quickly filled by talking…and if the teacher doesn't fill the silence, the student might.

Elephants

In order to get into the habit of pausing a little longer after a student has finished speaking, try counting elephants under your breath, i.e. one elephant, two elephants, three elephants and so on. You will only need to do it for a couple of weeks before you are leaving longer pauses without having to make a conscious effort. There is no absolute rule – different situations require different length pauses – but a sensible rule of thumb would be to aim for around three elephants.

Providing more dots

- Change the way students are grouped

- Present the information in a different way

- Help students reword their thinking

- Give some examples and invite students to add their own

- Model – work through an issue to show students how it is done. This process is enhanced when we ask them to describe aloud what we are doing as we demonstrate. It can also be helpful to pose questions to sharpen student's observation: *What did I do first?…What happened when I…?* And so on.

- Modelling is not limited to the teacher; other students can be used to demonstrate how something is done: *Watch Louise do that and describe to me what you notice.*

- Help students clarify their thinking: *you said…can you tell me what you meant by that?*

- Ask students:

  - *What evidence or examples can you give to show me your thinking?*
  - *What further information do you need to make sense of this?*
  - *What does a person who understands this know that you don't?*
  - *What question would you like to ask at this point?*
  - *Tell me what you do know?*
  - *Which is the most important?*
  - *Have you ever done anything like this before?*
  - *What does it remind you of?*
  - *Can you tell me what the answer isn't? What can we rule out?*
  - *Give me an answer (as opposed to the answer).*
  - *Give me three possible answers. Which is the most likely? Why?*

Step two: decide whether or not to intervene

- Do I need to intervene at this point – is it necessary?
- Would it be intervention or interference?
- Do I need to intervene with an individual, a small group or with the whole class?

> **AFL**
>
> When a child says something or asks a question that suggests a serious misunderstanding, the first thought of the teacher must be, *is the misunderstanding limited to the individual or shared by all / the majority of the group?* It is worth taking the trouble to find out.

Keep in mind *what am I trying to achieve? Am I holding their motivation and interest levels? How long have I got?* In reality, the decision about whether or not to intervene will be inextricably linked with the third step…

Step three: decide upon the nature of your intervention

Intervention does not mean telling them the answer, giving them your understanding or providing them with the completed picture. Rather, intervention involves providing more dots – clues or pointers – that will help unblock their thinking. Staying with the dots metaphor, the thought process that will be taking place may well be:

- Do they need more dots?
- Is the gap between the dots too large?
- Is the gap too small?
- Are the dots in the right place?
- Do they need *part* of the picture?
- Do they need a different kind of dot?

When we talk about intervention, many people immediately think of students who are struggling. However, it is equally important for teachers to be aware of and intervene with students who are coasting and finding the work lacks challenge.

After – reflecting on the picture

There is an old adage – you learn from experience; however, it only holds water if that experience is reflected upon. There is a correlation here with classroom practice, for as much as active engagement and experience are essential components, a learning experience is only complete when the activity is reflected upon and the learning consolidated.

Students are:	leads to:	teacher mode:
Passive	Knowing	Instruction
Active	Understanding	
Reflective	Deeper understanding	Facilitation

A helpful rule of thumb for teachers is: activity will take children so far; activity and reflection will take them further.

Consolidation

Consider the diagram opposite; when children are *passive* they are receiving information without having to think too much about it. The fact that they may be on task, completing their work neatly and even answering questions correctly can be misleading and misconstrued as learning. It is the *receive, retain, regurgitate* model of information transmission that will, at best, lead to *knowing*.

To make sense of information, learners have to do something with it – they have to be *active*. Active in this sense refers to cognitively rather than physically active and simply means that children have to think about the information they encounter. There are no guarantees in learning but interrogating and manipulating information – reducing it, changing it and so on – will make it more likely that children *begin* to understand it.

Begin is the key word here, for although actively engaging with information will develop *an* understanding, this understanding will be enhanced and taken to a deeper level by reflecting upon the experience. In the classroom, it simply means giving children a little time to consider – at a conscious level – what they are learning and taking away from an activity. It is this *pause and ponder* approach that enables children to *clarify and consolidate* their thinking. A helpful rule of thumb for teachers therefore is: activity will take children so far; activity *and* reflection, however, will take them further.

It is important to acknowledge that, although activity and reflection have been divided for the purposes of this section, the distinction is somewhat arbitrary, for the two are inextricably linked – the warp and the weft of the complex tapestry that is learning. It is also important to point out that learning comes quite naturally to human beings; we were learning quite nicely before schools came along – the challenge for the teacher is to manage this complex and instinctive process within the context and constraints of the classroom.

> I find the Magenta Principles a simple and effective method of promoting self-reflection in my students. Using and tailoring different principles gives plenaries throughout the lesson variety and value. After explaining complex concepts during lessons, designing reflection activities using different Magenta Principles allows me to effectively see how much students have understood.
>
> Simon Hall
> *Science teacher, Whitley Bay High School*

Which word best describes the children you teach?

- Passive

- Active

- Reflective

Reflection is often neglected

It is probably fair to suggest that the word teachers are least likely to use to describe their students is *reflective*. Put another way, if we think of learning as a giant, complicated jigsaw comprising numerous interlinked and interconnected pieces, it is safe to suggest that if the picture is incomplete in any way, the piece most likely to be missing is reflection.

There are a number of contributory factors why this is so:

1   Teachers take too long at the beginning of a lesson
2   Lessons have speeded up
3   Activity is greatly prized
4   Teachers are unsure what reflection 'looks like'.

Teachers take too long at the beginning of a lesson

Apply the ***dentist test*** to your teaching. A boy enters the classroom 10 minutes after the lesson has begun. He apologises and explains that he has been to the dentist. *Don't worry*, replies the teacher, *you haven't missed anything.*

Many lessons are slow to get going and are often characterised by what are little more than teaching rituals that do little or nothing to promote learning. These largely wasted minutes at the beginning are the reason why so many teachers run out of time towards the end. Of course, reflecting and consolidating learning are not confined to the end of the experience – the best teachers weave reflection throughout the entire lesson; however, it is important to consolidate learning as a lesson draws to a conclusion and wasted minutes at the beginning often prevent teachers from doing this properly.

This is not to say that the beginning of a lesson is unimportant – helping students make connections and place the lesson in a wider context contribute in no small way to helping them learn. The question mark, however, is whether the amount of time we spend at the beginning is proportionate to the overall contribution the introduction makes to learning.

In order to leave sufficient time for meaningful reflection, try planning your lessons backwards – or ***Christmas dinner planning.*** With your Christmas dinner you decide what time you want to eat and work backwards to determine what time you need to start cooking the vegetables and so on. Do the same with your lesson; decide how much time you need for reflection and work backwards.

Learning – not pace or activity – must be our focus, for pace without productivity is meaningless; activity for activity's sake is superficial.

Lessons have speeded up

There is little doubt that the speed of lessons has increased significantly in recent years. This is largely due to an Ofsted-fuelled obsession with pace, based upon the erroneous and simplistic assumption that quicker is somehow better. It isn't. In fact, it can be argued that the pace in the majority of lessons is far too fast with far too little emphasis given to allowing children to pause, reflect, consider and consolidate.

This is not to say that pace isn't important or an excuse for teachers to be casual and students to be lackadaisical; it is simply an observation that we must be wary of the pendulum effect and that where once many lessons lacked pace we have now swung to the other extreme and many lessons are simply too fast.

It is not pace we seek but *appropriate* pace. As Bucks Fizz once suggested, *you've got to speed it up and then you've got to slow it down!* The best teachers have known this all along, recognising that there needs to be episodes of activity – when the pace is high – punctuated by periods of reflection – when the pace needs to drop – so that learning can be consolidated. And learning – not pace or activity – must be our focus, for pace without productivity is meaningless; activity for activity's sake is superficial.

Activity is greatly prized

The teaching profession greatly values activity. Teachers frequently talk about a buzz in the classroom – and other teachers know exactly what they mean. Where once we prized silence, now we prize activity.

Indeed, we value activity to the extent that we worry if children are – or appear to be – inactive. And this is a significant part of the problem; for while it is relatively easy to identify students being active in the classroom, it is much harder to distinguish between a child in passive and reflective mode. Reflective looks very much like passive – which in turn looks suspiciously like inactive.

There is an old saying, not everything of value can be measured and not everything that can be measured is of value, and in some respects the profession is guilty of valuing something simply because it is possible to identify and quantify it. Spotting children on task is straightforward; distinguishing between the child deep in reflection and the daydreamer is infinitely more challenging.

In other words, while it is possible to spot children *working*, it is much more difficult, if not impossible, to spot children *learning.*

There are teachers who know they're required to do a plenary and there are teachers who **understand what this means...**

... and there are implications here for professional development.

Teachers are unsure of what reflection 'looks like'

Teachers will often claim that the reason that reflection is so often neglected is because they are required to cram so much into a lesson they often run out of time at the end. There may be an element of truth in this, however; at least as significant is that fact that a great many teachers are unsure of what reflection looks like.

The adoption of the word *plenary* into the professional vocabulary has done little to help. On the contrary, the word is the source of myth, confusion and angst, and has arguably done more harm than good. It is not the concept of a plenary that is the problem, more the word itself and the language that surrounds it. Consider how the word is used and it is apparent that it is associated with the teacher *doing*. For example, teachers are required to *do* a plenary; teachers are chastised if they fail to *do* a plenary; and so on.

Change the word and we get a completely different picture. Ask a teacher if there is a need for children to *consolidate* what they have just learned and you will invariably get a positive reply; ask them whether they need to do a *plenary* and you will get a very different response. Not only do we get a different response but it reveals a very different perspective on who is doing the doing. Children consolidate their learning by reflecting on it – it is a process that cannot be done to them, only by them.

The word plenary comes from the Latin word *plenus* and actually means *all to attend/full*. It offers no guidance to teachers whatsoever. There is a simple solution – stop using the word! Replace the word plenary with words such as *consolidate, reflect, demonstrate* or *review*, however, and teachers have a clear indicator about both purpose and practice. It would not guarantee that it would happen but by making explicit reference to reflection and consolidation we would make it more likely (see page 183).

There would be an additional benefit from dropping the word plenary as a great many teachers mistakenly assume that word means *at the end of*, or words to that effect. It has already been suggested that reflection is not – at least should not be – confined to the end of the lesson, but should be woven throughout the entire experience and by replacing the word plenary with reflection we would increase the likelihood of this taking place across a greater number of classrooms.

Quite simply there are teachers who know they're supposed to do a plenary and others who understand what this means…and there are implications here for professional development.

It is no coincidence that the schools with the best professional development programmes invariably have the best teaching and learning.

Implications for CPD

The best teachers get it; their understanding of their role goes deeper than knowing where the boxes are and how to tick them. The best leaders also get it; their understanding of professional development goes beyond making sure teachers know where the boxes are and have whatever is required to ensure they are ticked. In the same way that the best teachers are acutely aware that facilitating learning requires more than simply telling, the best leaders understand that professional development involves more than training.

Perhaps most significantly, the best teachers understand learning. They appreciate it is a messy, complex, even mysterious process, and to facilitate it in others requires the ability to respond, adapt and intervene. As has been suggested from the outset, great teachers are flexible and can think on their feet; certainly they plan lessons but they also have plans B, C and D up their sleeve and the confidence and judgement to know when to use them.

In short, the very best teachers have **professional capacity.** It follows therefore that any genuine aspirations of excellence must be accompanied with and underpinned by a commitment to consciously develop such capacity. The very best leaders appreciate this. They are aware that their role goes beyond providing training and tips. Their role is to facilitate *professional learning*… and facilitation goes way beyond telling.

Thinking of professional development in terms of professional learning puts a very different complexion on things. For the consistent message throughout this book – and the underpinning philosophy that has shaped all of the ideas in it – has been that:

- Learning is the consequence of thinking
- Language is central to learning
- Learning is an active process.

The implications are crystal clear; in order to learn teachers need to be thinking, talking and doing.

In many respects, *professional dialogue* is the key for when teachers regularly and routinely discuss and debate professional issues in an honest, reflective manner their individual and collective understanding deepens. The challenge for those responsible for professional development in schools is simple – get them talking!

To be precise, teachers need to be talking openly and honestly; guarded, *ah but*, conversations that essentially seek to justify the status quo will not suffice. The challenge is to remove – or at least reduce – the emotion, for emotion is the barrier to reflection. In simple terms, human beings become defensive when they perceive

For too long teachers have been given the **answers;** in these exercises they are required to grapple with the questions. For many, initially at least, it can be an uncomfortable process.

attack. This in turn has ramifications for the way we seek to instigate professional conversations. For example, conversations that begin with teachers receiving feedback from a lesson observation – however skilfully and objectively it is done – will inevitably lead to an emotional response. Removing or reducing the emotion necessitates that we remove the judgement. We therefore require an alternative, non-judgemental catalyst for professional discussion such as the use of tools, information, video and experiences outlined in this section.

It is an approach to professional development that, in many respects, is the inverse of what has emerged as the dominant model of school improvement in recent years, namely place teachers under ever-increasing pressure. Although it may be counterintuitive, resist the temptation to dismiss the approach as weak and ineffective. On the contrary, the ideas outlined in this section are challenging, not least because they are unfamiliar. For too long teachers have been given the answers; in these exercises they are required to grapple with the questions. For many, initially at least, it can be an uncomfortable process.

There is no suggestion that the training, monitoring and feedback approach to school improvement that features so prominently in so many schools does not have a place. It does; however, it is an approach that is more likely to produce consistency and compliance rather than develop capacity. It may well result in competent teaching but will not necessarily lead to wow learning. At the beginning of the book it was suggested that while all teachers want to help students pass exams, there were some that wanted more; *they want children to get it, get why they got it and, as much as anything enjoy the process.* The same is true of school leaders; all of them want their staff to pass the Ofsted test but some want more; they want to develop teachers who have the ability to enthrall, engage and excite.

The Magenta Principles are not a collection of resources or activities. Rather, they represent a range of ideas designed to get students talking, thinking and doing in order to help them develop a deeper understanding. The approach to professional development as outlined in this section is underpinned by exactly the same philosophy – simply substitute the word teacher for student.

They do not represent a comprehensive coverage of all aspects of professional development – that is beyond the scope of this book – rather, they focus upon two dimensions that are fundamental to the Magenta Principles approach, namely facilitation and reflection.

Instruction		Facilitation

0   10

Which is the best-fit word – instruction or facilitation?

If instruction is 0 and facilitation 10, which number best represents the teacher's approach? (Don't allow people to sit on the fence and say 5.)

The bookends technique works with any pair of words such as:

occupied..................... engaged
knowing...................... understanding
passive .... active
boring.......................... fun
predictable................ unusual

Developing facilitation skills

Bookends

Step one

This is best done using a short video but can also be adapted to be used during a lesson observation. Play 2–3 minutes of the clip and then pause. Which word best describes the role of the teacher? Were they *instructing* or were they *facilitating?*

It can be effective to deliberately choose a clip that is likely to lead to some disagreement and therefore generate some discussion. Do not allow teachers to sit on the fence – which is the best-fit word, instruction or facilitation?

A variation is to use the spectrum scale shown in the diagram opposite. Place the two words instruction and facilitation at the extreme ends of the spectrum. If instruction is 0 and facilitation 10, what number best represents the teacher's approach in the video clip? Do not allow the number 5 – number 5 is the fence!

Every individual writes down a number and then shares it with the group. Is there a consensus or a wide disagreement? Are all of the numbers above or below 5 or do we have a range of numbers from either side of the fence? Are the numbers from the extreme ends of the spectrum or are they clustered around the middle?

Step two

Consider what was it about the teacher's behaviour that suggested to you that they were instructing/facilitating. Can we identify a range of indicators that we can look for and consider?

For example:

- How does the teacher respond to a question? (With an answer or with a question?)
- Who is doing the majority of the talking – teacher or student?
- Is the emphasis on knowing or understanding?
- Who is using the word *because* – teacher or student?
- Are there pauses and periods of silence?
- What types of questions is the teacher asking – open or closed?
- Is the teacher *bouncing* an idea around the group/class?
- Is the teacher intervening or interfering?

Can we make connections between some of the words/phrases that we are using in our discussion? Divide the words/phrases that we are using into two piles; those we would most associate with instruction and those we would most associate with facilitation. For example, would we most associate *knowing* with facilitation or instruction?

I've never really thought about teaching and learning at this depth before and I couldn't believe how much we got from such a short video clip. All the time I was thinking about my lessons and how I respond.

This activity has had an immediate impact on my teaching, as where I may have told children answers I often now respond with a question or open their question out to the wider class. It's amazing how much more I get from the children just by holding back a little.

Rachel Hayward
Year 2/3 teacher

Step three

Watch the clip again. This time pause the video at every key moment and consider the indicators that we have just discussed.

For example, a child asks a question. Pause the video and consider how might the teacher respond – with an answer *or* with a question? With an answer *and* a question? Consider how a teacher might respond if they were in instructor/facilitator mode.

Play the clip on – how did the teacher respond?

Step four

Teachers revisit the instructor/facilitator spectrum and have an opportunity to change their number (0–10).

- How many change their number as a result of a deeper analysis?
- Are the revised numbers higher/lower than the original number?
- Do we now have a consensus view as to whether the teacher is instructing/facilitating?

Step five

What do you take away from this exercise?

Being a fairly experienced teacher, I was convinced that I could spot the difference between instruction and facilitation a mile off: instruction is me talking; facilitation is letting them do the talking. The activities that we did with Mike surprised me and made me rethink my sweeping generalisation. Thinking about it in a little more depth, I realised I'd been fooled by instruction masquerading as facilitation. I think I learnt that the key to doing either effectively is having a clear idea of what you want the students to take away from the lesson and how you want them to have discovered and explored it. I discovered that I needed to be more creative (and planned!) to facilitate but it was worth it as they learnt things I didn't expect them too as well as the things I did.

Katie Spurr
St Thomas More School, Blaydon-upon-Tyne

We asked all of our teachers to teach a few lessons outside of their curriculum area – it certainly got them talking! One experience was particularly interesting when a student claimed that the lesson was the best maths lesson they'd ever had. When the teacher – a linguist – expressed her surprise on the grounds that she didn't understand maths, the student responded with the memorable comment, *nor do we!*

We tried to unpack this a little further and it became increasingly obvious that while some teachers endeavoured to develop understanding in their students, there were others who spent the lesson demonstrating their own.

Not only did this incident trigger a huge amount of debate, looking back, it was one of the pivotal moments in our drive to improve the quality of teaching and learning in the school.

Mike Hughes
Secondary Deputy Head 1994

Teach in contrasting styles

An effective follow-up experience to the best-fit word activity is to teach a lesson, or part of a lesson, in two contrasting styles, predominantly as an instructor and predominantly as a facilitator.

There are many variations around the theme. For example, teach the same lesson in different styles to parallel groups/teach a section of a lesson as an instructor before teaching the next section as a facilitator/be in instructor mode when working with one group but be more of a facilitator with another.

The aim of the exercise is to be conscious of the two approaches and to force teachers to think very carefully about the differences between instruction and facilitation – what do they need to do more of, less of and so on. It works best when teachers do not go to the extreme ends of the instructor/facilitator spectrum; be a little more instructional in the first lesson while making a conscious effort to be more facilitative in the second.

Teach outside of your specialism

As a general rule, the more people know about something the more likely it is they will talk. In the context of teaching, the more a teacher knows about a subject the more likely it is they will instruct.

When they teach a lesson outside of their specialism they are put in a position where they cannot instruct – because they don't have the necessary expertise – and are forced to facilitate.

It is a simple exercise and yet it is a professional development experience that will generate much reflection and discussion. And, as with the other ideas in this section, it is the thought process and conversations that are provoked by the experience, which is the key to helping teachers develop a deeper professional understanding.

The exercises outlined above can be powerful learning experiences in their own right but the reflective process will be enhanced and the impact will be greater if the lessons are filmed. Not only does this allow the teacher to watch the lesson over again they have the option of sharing the clips with colleagues. Reflecting upon an experience alone will take you so far; discussing it with others is likely to take you further.

Recording the experience also opens up the possibility of using some of the tools such as the bookends activity outlined on page 169.

During our work with Mike on the Magenta Principles he has continually stressed the need to ensure that the focus is on learning rather than activity. In order to reinforce this point we decided to use some video clips as part of our CPD programme in order to help all staff grasp what this 'looked like' in practice.

We asked a couple of outstanding teachers to film themselves twice using the same Magenta Principle activity. Their brief was to use the activity competently in the first clip and then fully exploit the potential of the activity in the second clip by using high quality facilitation skills.

The CPD activity was exceptionally well received by staff. Over and over again, people referred to how both teachers 'drew out the learning' in the second clip. The need to 'draw out learning' is a phrase that teachers had heard before but had not necessarily seen. The discussions about precisely how the teachers did this gave everyone a real insight into what we actually mean by facilitation skills.

Abigail Lear
Vice Principal, Lutterworth College

Constraint lesson

Constraint exercises are common in sport – you are only allowed to hit backhands, use your left foot and so on.

In this exercise, we place a constraint on the teacher for a lesson or part of a lesson. For example:

- The teacher is only allowed to answer a question with a question – the idea being to stop the teacher immediately diving in with the answer and going into instructor mode.
- The teacher is only allowed to talk in response to a question from a student. It takes a few minutes for students to get the hang of this but when they do the result is genuine student-led learning.
- The teacher is only allowed to talk for a maximum of 10 – or five – minutes. This doesn't mean that the teacher gives the students an exercise and instructs them to get on with it – it means they have to think very carefully about how to use their talk time to maximum effect.
- The teacher is only allowed to ask a total of four questions – the idea being to focus their attention on quality not quantity.

Video clips

It can be helpful for teachers to see what facilitation looks like and one of the easiest ways of doing this is to collect a series of with and without clips. Film a short (5–15-minute) clip of a teacher using one of the Magenta Principles without facilitation/with poor facilitation skills. Film the same teacher using the same Magenta Principle exercise but this time facilitating the experience.

Use the clips in small groups to stimulate discussion – what was different? What did they do more of/less of? What was the impact on student learning? Which clip is more representative of the way you teach? Providing we have chosen appropriate clips, teachers will almost certainly be able to see that the second clip was better as the teacher was facilitating effectively. However, it is the process of articulating their thoughts and making the differences between the clips explicit that will help teachers develop their own practice.

As ever, finish the exercise with:

- What are you taking away from this experience?
- What will you do differently as a result?

RAP Wall

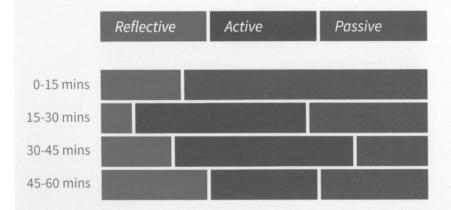

The dialogue that resulted from using the RAP wall enabled us to develop a shared appreciation of how to move students from activity and knowledge towards a deeper understanding. *(see page 191)*

Shenley Brook End School

Developing reflective learners

RAP walls

These can be used during lesson observations but are most effective when used with video clips of lessons. A suggested approach is as follows:

Step one: working in small groups (four to eight) watch a video clip of a lesson (around five minutes).

Step two: consider which word best sums up the students (as learners) – passive, active, reflective?

Step three: you have 12 marks to allocate to the three words to best represent the students. You may allocate all 12 marks to one word, divide them between two or divide them between three.

> For example: if you feel the students have been totally passive, you might decide to go:

Reflective	0	Active	0	Passive	12

> If you feel they have been some way between passive and active but there hasn't been any reflection, you might decide to go:

Reflective	0	Active	6	Passive	6

> If you feel that while there were moments of passivity the majority have largely been active with an element of reflection, you might allocate the 12 marks as:

Reflective	3	Active	7	Passive	2

> Complete the first bar on the diagram accordingly.

Step four: share your allocation with other members of the group. Do you agree? Through discussion, try to reach a consensus view.

Step five: discuss the kind of things that you are looking for that might indicate a student is/students are being passive, active and so on.

Step six: watch the next five minutes of the lesson and repeat the process.

Individually and/or collectively, complete your diagram bar by bar so you end up with your *RAP wall*. It is important to emphasise that the RAP wall is simply a tool to help teachers reflect on practice and is designed to stimulate discussion and debate. It should be used not as a one-off event but as part of an ongoing process.

Zone of challenge

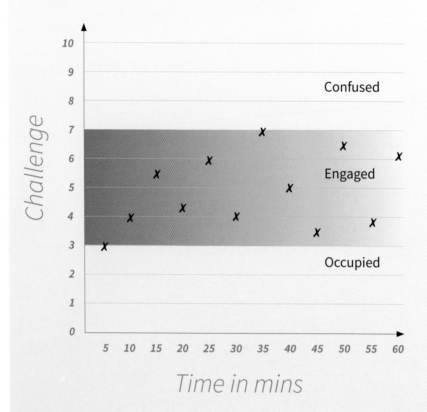

The fact that using the Zone of Challenge grid raises a series of questions rather than providing a list of answers is significant and entirely in keeping with the philosophy of facilitating professional learning rather than providing training. As was suggested on page 167, teachers have often been provided with the answers, in this approach they have to grapple with the questions. It is not without irony that this is a challenging process.

Zone of challenge

All teachers have been told that they must engage and challenge students, yet how many teachers have had the opportunity to explore what that actually means? The Zone of Challenge grid (opposite), which was first published in *And the Main Thing is… Learning*, was designed to help teachers to do just that.

The idea is simple; as you watch a lesson, pause at regular intervals (every few minutes) and reflect upon the level of challenge experienced by students. While it is not possible to produce an objective analysis of a lesson, it will get teachers reflecting upon and discussing practice, which in turn will help clarify and deepen their understanding.

The Zone of Challenge grid can be used in many ways:

- As a reflective tool after the lesson
- As a planning tool before the lesson
- By teachers
- By students – it is always interesting to compare the teacher's perception of challenge with the student's perception
- In real-time or in conjunction with video
- By a teacher working as an individual or by a group of teachers working collaboratively.

It is a simple tool that has the potential to generate sophisticated discussion. The fact that the complex, nebulous nature of challenge defies capture on a graph is entirely the point. Completing the grid is not the objective; professional dialogue is.

A great many schools and teachers have used the Zone of Challenge grid in the last few years – an account of how the tool has been used by Shenley Brook End School can be found on pages 189-193 – and a number of key issues and questions have emerged.

- What does challenge look like in different subjects? Is challenge in maths different to challenge in PE?
- How quickly do we challenge our students at the beginning of lessons? Are lessons slow to start? Do we pass the dentist test? (see page 159)
- Do we challenge all students? Are these the same people every lesson?
- How do we challenge students at the end of the lesson? Is it appropriate to be challenging students at the end of the lesson? Should reflection be challenging?
- Is it possible to challenge students for an entire lesson? How do we sustain challenge?

Teacher talk / Learner talk

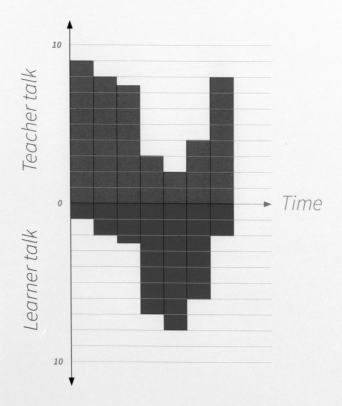

This tool can be used when observing a lesson or watching a film of a lesson. Simply pause every 5 minutes and consider who was doing the talking – teacher or students. You have 10 marks to award to reflect the balance of teacher talk – learner talk.

Teacher talk/learner talk

Mike's early (whole staff) training sessions at Whitley Bay had a significant impact because of the way he explored with us notions of the teacher as a facilitator of learning. His visual representation of teacher talk (highlighted in red) in a lesson juxtaposed with student talk (highlighted in blue) helped us map our own lesson plans. This culminated in a moment of revelation: our most outstandingly effective teachers were inclined to talk less, (specifically in the opening ten minutes of the lesson, and question more). Our challenge was to ensure all teachers moved their lessons from red to blue, and in Mike's Magenta Principles we found a simple and effective way of helping them do this.

Whitley Bay High School

Although it is something of a generalisation, the best teachers tend to talk less. Similarly, the assertion that many teachers talk more than they realise will resonate with many. Even those who are sceptical of these claims would be hard pressed to deny that teacher talk is a key contributory factor to learning, or lack of learning, in a lesson. To that end, exploring the balance between teacher talk and learner talk can therefore be a powerful and effective professional development activity.

And exploring it is the key, for this is a complex issue and we must guard against the pendulum effect – teachers who once spent the entire lesson lecturing now say next to nothing because that is the latest fashion. While the *best teachers talk less* is a useful rule of thumb, we must remember that talking has a place! What we seek is both a balance and a deep understanding of the impact our talking has on their learning.

The grid opposite is another example of how a simple tool can be the catalyst for sophisticated dialogue and offers the opportunity to move the debate beyond the simplistic issue of quantity and into the subtleties of the facilitation process. For example, many people focus upon the *amount* of teacher talk. While this is undoubtedly significant, equally significant is the *pattern* of teacher talk; a teacher may talk for a total of 20 minutes, but do they do this in one block? Do they front-load the lesson with a lengthy period of exposition before they engage students in a task or do they immerse the children in an activity before helping them unpack it? There are more questions than answers – and that is exactly how it should be.

The sequence of professional development activities on the opposite page employs a number of the Magenta Principles to enable teachers to reflect upon the whole issue of reflection.

Step two ....replace
Step three.......arrange
Step four ....contrast
Step five ....connect
Step six............connect

These activities are designed to get teachers thinking, talking and doing in order to deepen their professional understanding and develop their professional capacity.

Where facilitation meets reflection

Step one: what does the word plenary mean? Write down the dictionary definition of the word plenary. Note: it is important to stress we are looking for the dictionary definition of the word.

Very few teachers know what the word actually means. The more you think about this the more bizarre it becomes! (The answer can be found on page 163.)

Note: the point being made here is that using the word plenary in the context of teaching and learning is both inappropriate and ineffective as it does little to guide teachers as to what they are trying to achieve in this phase of the lesson. This point is discussed in more detail on page 163.

Step two: replace the word plenary with a word/phrase that better captures what we are trying to achieve during this phase of the lesson.

If teachers are struggling to grasp the task it can be helpful to give them a prompt. For example, you might think the period of the lesson that we refer to as the plenary is when you want to help students *review* their learning – or *demonstrate* their learning – so that you can *assess* their learning and so on.

Step three: which is the best/most appropriate word to use instead of the word plenary? Use the words and phrases generated in step two to complete either a diamond nine or an archery target (see page 98).

A variation is to give teachers words to use in this exercise such as: *review, reflect, demonstrate, assess, consolidate, summarise, extend, recap, digest.*

Step four: what is the difference between summarise and reflect?

Note: we are trying to highlight the difference between the teacher summarising what the students have done and the students reflecting upon what they have learned.

Step five: watch a short clip of the last 10–15 minutes of a lesson. Which word best describes the clip – summarise or reflect?

This exercise can be enhanced and extended using the bookends tool described on page 169.

Step six: think about a lesson that you taught recently. Which word best describes they way the lesson ended – summarise or reflect?

Extend this line of thinking: which word – summarise or reflect – best describes a typical ending of one of your lessons. How can a teacher switch the emphasis from summarise to reflect? What do they need to do differently? What do they need to do more or less of? Is it ever appropriate to summarise? If so, when?

I announced at our morning briefing that all staff would move classrooms 15 minutes before the end of period 3 and conduct a plenary for a lesson they hadn't taught.

Shortly afterwards I received a visit from one of the 'staffroom personalities' who informed me that, in his opinion, the idea was ridiculous. He went on to say that the announcement had caused *a bit of a stir* in the prep room and how *everyone is talking about why it won't work and what teachers need to know about the lesson in order to conduct a plenary.* It was all pretty animated and he finished the tirade with the claim that *it will never work!*

Bearing in mind that the aim of the exercise is to get teachers talking, I replied, *it already has* – and shut the door!

Secondary Deputy Head

Switched plenaries

In a nutshell, this activity involves teachers conducting a plenary for a lesson they have not taught.

It is a variation on the teaching outside of your specialism exercise when teachers are put in a position where they can't instruct – because they do not have the necessary subject knowledge. In this scenario teachers are put in a position where they cannot summarise what the students have done because they genuinely don't know! They can, however, facilitate their reflections on what they have learned. The exercise is most effective when we combine these dimensions – i.e. teachers lead a plenary for a lesson they haven't taught outside of their subject specialism.

It is a simple idea yet hugely effective at getting teachers to talk and think about practice and, providing we give some thought to safety considerations in particular subjects, it is easy – and cheap – to organise. Indeed, just announcing the activity will provoke a reaction among staff!

Switching the emphasis of professional development

It is no coincidence that the schools with the best teaching and learning are also the schools with the best professional development programmes. For the relationship between what we do with teachers and what teachers in turn do with students is strong and when our interpretation of professional development is limited to a training and telling approach, don't be surprised if this is mirrored in the classroom. If, however, our professional development is based upon a culture of exploration and dialogue and is specifically geared towards developing a deeper understanding, then there is every chance this will be reflected in pedagogy. The message is simple: if we want active and reflective students we must begin by developing active and reflective teachers.

The ideas and activities outlined in this section represent a fundamental switch in emphasis of professional development from an event to an experience; from teachers being trained to teachers learning about learning; from a *done to* model to a *done by* model. It reflects a mindset and a culture that has the potential to pervade the entire school from staffroom to classroom.

The RAP principle on page 177 was originally conceived to help teachers reflect upon classroom practice. However, it can also be used to reflect upon the nature and efficacy of our approach to professional development.

The relationship between what we do with teachers and what teachers in turn do with students is strong and when our interpretation of professional development is limited to a training and telling approach, don't be surprised if this is mirrored in the classroom.

Passive

When teachers attend a twilight inset – 10 top tips for plenaries – they receive some strategies that could be used in a plenary. In events of this kind, teachers are largely passive and will leave the event knowing additional activities they could use. As a result, we may get greater variety at the end of lessons.

Apply a Magenta Principle and reduce this paragraph to the key words and we arguably end up with *passive, receive, event, knowing and variety.*

Active

On the other hand, when teachers participate in a switched plenary exercise (see page 185), they are active. While there are no guarantees of course, we have opened up the possibility that as a result of the experience, they have a deeper understanding of facilitating the reflective process and as a result we get greater depth at the end of lessons.

The key words now become *active, experience, understanding and depth.*

Reflective

However, the activity itself will only take people so far – the experience is only completed when teachers reflect upon it. This process can be enhanced if the switched plenary has been filmed. One potentially powerful professional development experience is to compare a video clip of you conducting a plenary for a lesson you have taught with the way you facilitate a switch plenary. What are you doing differently, what are you doing more of/less of? Which word best sums up the clips – summarise or reflect?

Professional reflection

As with all professional development exercises/experiences, it is important to end with:

- What are you taking away from this exercise?
- What will you do differently as a result?

In the same way that teachers facilitate learning, the onus is on those responsible for professional development to facilitate professional learning. The activity or experience – whether it be for students in the classroom or teachers in the staffroom – is only as effective as the facilitation. At the risk of being repetitive, there are implications here for those responsible for professional development…but that's another book.

It was the simple nature of the tools with their **profound capacity to promote reflection and professional dialogue** in such a refreshing way that was at the heart of the drive to change the internal culture of the school.

Chris Holmwood
Senior Deputy Head, Shenley Brook End School

Shenley Brook End – changing the culture

The story begins with an Ofsted inspection in which we were judged, as was possible at this time, to be an outstanding school but only graded good for teaching and learning. The advice from the HMI was that if we wanted to move teaching and learning from good to great we needed to *lift the lid* and, intriguingly, *to tweak the interface between teaching* and learning.

On reading Mike's book *Tweak to Transform,* it struck me how much our emphasis in the classroom had become about delivery rather than exploration and that the implications for professional development were to be challenging if we were to make this transition of approach across our classrooms. Using a number of his tools and ideas we took a strategic approach to using staff development to effect cultural change with a key emphasis upon using deliberately non-Ofsted lesson planning and observation tools to encourage reflective practice. We quickly found that this shift away from a traditional culture of Ofsted judgements towards a more developmental approach had an impact upon encouraging teachers' own thinking to develop their own professional capacity and led to more sustainable and authentic improvements in their practice. The simple nature of the tools with their profound capacity to promote reflection and professional dialogue in such a refreshing way was at the heart of these approaches.

The RAP wall tool (see page 177) was first trialled in our Maths team and then launched as a project across the school. Staff reflected upon how much passive, active and reflective learning occurred within their own lessons and across their team. They discussed the differences between how those types of learning actually looked in lessons. They considered which styles of learning predominated at the start of topics and in revision. They then began to create a shared vision of how they would like passive, active and reflective learning to look in their particular subject. This was important as it moved teachers beyond the simplistic assumption that passive learning is necessarily bad and active learning good. It created dialogue around the need for balance and the need to plan for these different modes of learning, especially so that reflective learning could become more explicitly increased as it became clear that this was the area that generally became most squeezed.

As cross-curricular discussions took place, the dialogue and reflection around similarities and differences proved really illuminating. It encouraged staff to experiment with new ways of understanding the depth of learning occurring. One such approach was called *Switch Plenaries,* during which teachers moved into the end of each other's lessons. We found that finishing off each other's lessons

The visual style of the process and its intrinsic subjectivity were key in stimulating and supporting the discussion and reflection.

Chris Holmwood
Shenley Brook End School

encouraged more reflection time for students and helped staff assess and then share the depth of learning they had gleaned through their end of lesson questioning. The RAP wall seemed to be opening classroom doors in other ways.

Teams learned from each other and tried new things in order to address such aspects as the way in which using the RAP wall really brought home the extent to which practical subjects had particularly passive starts and ends to lessons. Similarly, the RAP wall revealed that theoretical subjects often rushed into active learning but did not always provide the reflective time for consolidation. Developmental lesson observations that were being used to promote staff learning and reflection rather than being organised for the purposes of Ofsted feedback were clearly not only having an impact upon the teacher being observed but also upon the colleague observing. Dialogue across the subjects assisted the creation of a shared understanding of how to move students from activity and knowledge towards a deeper understanding of their learning; encouraging the development of reflective teachers was also developing reflective learners.

There was quite a level of professional argument and debate about how to define the three areas of passive, active and reflective at all, and the subjectivity around this actually raised the level of reflection and debate significantly. For example, if a student is reading chapter one of *Animal Farm*, is that passive, active or reflective learning? We came to the conclusion that we couldn't tell for sure, but we could consciously guide the type of learning by the way we framed that activity. Moving from *Read the first chapter of Animal Farm* to *Read the first chapter of Animal Farm and then tell me about anything it reminds you about what you learned in History last week* is a good example. So the *RAP wall* began to change teachers' planning, lesson structure, the framing of activities and the language and especially the quality of questioning being used.

The RAP wall was not the only tool that contributed to this improvement. We ran a similar project using the *Zone of Challenge* tool. The use of this developed slowly and organically, with suggestions for improvement in ways it could be used coming from all over the school and from teachers with very different levels of experience. This itself was an indication of how our professional development culture had been changed through the collaborative work we had done on RAP.

The Zone of Challenge evolved into being used in a number of ways, and as time went on these often overlapped so that lesson preparation, observation and reflection combined in a powerful way. We began by using it as an observation tool on which a colleague would record their perception of the level of challenge in a lesson. As with the RAP wall, the visual style of the process and its intrinsic

This experience has profoundly shaped both the professional development and leadership culture of the school.

subjectivity were key in stimulating and supporting the discussion and reflection, especially when used in a cross-curricular way where perceptions of what challenge actually looks like were up for debate!

It then became used as a planning tool through which teachers mapped out the highs and lows of challenge intended throughout the lesson. Again, the visual nature of this was useful, and it helped teachers to reflect upon the need to vary levels of challenge and which techniques would best achieve this. When being observed, teachers could then overlay a record of how they felt the reality of the lesson went and compare this with not only the shape of their planning on the grid but also compare both versions with the observer's record.

An interesting development was in the use of this with students, either in small groups, ability groups or whole classes. This was especially helpful in growing the understanding of teachers about the extent to which students felt challenged, as opposed to how the teacher had recorded or felt about the challenge provided. It also helped to look at how children of different abilities within or across groups or subjects responded to challenge. Once again, reflective teachers and learners were becoming more effective teachers and learners.

This experience has profoundly shaped both the professional development and leadership culture of the school. One illuminating comment from a teacher at this time was *this whole approach has really taken me back to the reasons I came into teaching.* Another said *my capacity to improve the quality of a lesson during the lesson itself has improved vastly.* It is fair to say that the lid had been lifted and the interface between teaching and learning well and truly tweaked. Ofsted agreed with this assertion; at our next inspection the HMI commented that *the quality of debate about pedagogy in this school is exceptional.* Teaching and learning was judged to be outstanding.

Chris Holmwood
Senior Deputy Head
Shenley Brook End School

There are many examples of exciting and effective developments to classroom practice that have been individual rather than institution driven.

Using the Magenta Principles

It is not reading a book that is important but what you do as a result. This book is no different and having read about the Magenta Principles, the next step is to use them. That is what every single teacher who has contributed to this book did; having been introduced to the Magenta Principles – usually in a workshop – they tried them out. More than that, they explored them; they developed and customised them; and, in doing so, they began to understand them in a way that enabled them to move from adopting a strategy to adapting a principle.

It is apparent that this has taken place at a variety of scales. At one end of the extreme there are schools – most notably Whitley Bay High School – that have taken a whole school approach to implementing and developing the Magenta Principles. In these schools, the Magenta Principles are used consciously and strategically as a framework to develop classroom practice. More than that, in Whitley Bay High School, the Magenta Principles are part of the culture – their culture – and permeate the very fabric of the school. Their story is told in greater detail on page 201.

On the other hand, there are individual teachers who have encountered the Magenta Principles and are using them to varying degrees in their classroom. They may be using them in a limited way, they may be the only teacher in the school using the approach, they may not make explicit reference to the phrase Magenta Principles, but nonetheless some of the ideas and techniques can be found in their classroom.

Certainly it is easier swimming with the tide, but there is no need to wait for your school to adopt the Magenta Principles before you give them a go. Developing your practice is your professional responsibility; a personal thing, not entirely dependent upon external influences and initiatives. Indeed, there are many examples of exciting and effective developments to classroom practice that have been individual rather than institution driven.

Start small. Take one of the ideas that you have read about in this book and give it a go. It might be a task or a solitary question; it might take up an entire lesson or just a few minutes; it might be that you create a new resource or adapt an existing activity. It doesn't matter; what matters is that you give it a go – and the quicker the better for the longer you leave it the less likely it is that you will actually do it!

If you do nothing else other than make a conscious effort to enquire which was the hardest or which was the most important sentence, you are on your way, and, as the saying goes, a journey of a thousand miles…

Colleagues soon realised how easily the Magenta Principles could be adapted and implemented as a philosophy underpinning their teaching.

Sidmouth CE Primary School

Sidmouth CE Primary School

In September 2102 we created a Teaching and Learning Team, comprising four lead teachers, who taught across the age range from EYFS to Y6. As individuals, we had one thing in common – an intrinsic desire to grow and develop as professionals. As a team, our brief was simple: support the development of teaching and learning across the school but to do so in a non-judgemental, non-threatening way.

Initially, we were all a little unsure of what to expect; we were given some additional non-contact time and worked closely alongside Mike Hughes, who helped us develop an approach to professional development that would be effective for our school.

Three distinct, yet interwoven, strands emerged:

- Coaching
- Video analysis
- The Magenta Principles.

Not top down

It was massively important that our colleagues saw us as supportive rather than judgemental. Although all teachers accept the need to improve, performance management and monitoring can sometimes feel of limited use. Not only can it be a stressful process, but feedback can often feel like criticism. When this happens, change is either rejected or accepted only at face value and any developments to practice are only skin deep.

We therefore consciously adopted a coaching approach working alongside staff in a supportive rather than judgemental role and our colleagues bought into the process as a result.

Video analysis

The video project ran alongside the introduction of the Magenta Principles, enhancing what was going on within classrooms. Teachers were invited – not told, which was important – to video themselves teaching and then to share part or all of what they had recorded, in pairs, with two members of the Teaching and Learning Team. Very few staff chose not to take the opportunity to be part of the project and the feedback we received was overwhelmingly positive. Staff were released from class to take part, and the sessions allowed for informal, non-judgemental dialogue and reflection to take place. The video project allowed us all to share experiences, ideas and concerns; we were relaxed and open enough to ask questions and voice fears in a 'safe' environment.

The Headteacher's perspective

There is no doubt that the work of the Teaching and Learning Team has been instrumental in helping improve the quality of teaching and learning throughout the school. In particular, it is apparent that:

- The Magenta Principles worked – where used they were successful in changing attitudes of either the teacher or the pupil. Often very subtle changes were seen in classes.

- Pupils become more articulate. The language of learning has changed in the classes, with children becoming very clear about what they are learning.

- The zone of challenge has changed – pupils would often try to do as much as they could, pick the easiest questions or rush a task. By adapting the tasks the children were soon picking more challenging activities or setting themselves new goals. The quality of work was often better.

- Pupils appeared to enjoy learning more – new methods of teaching similar tasks meant the children were engaged. They were often more empowered to take the lead in their own learning, usually setting their own personal challenges rather than wanting to do the same as a peer group.

- Many of the ideas developed worked across the whole school. Staff developed activities that could be used in any age group.

- The principles don't need to be used in isolation. We found that they often only filled part of a lesson, but that the shift in dialogue and focus was so great that it altered the course of the rest of the lesson.

Paul Walker
Headteacher
Sidmouth CE Primary School

Staff clearly appreciated the time to have these professional discussions. At first there was an understandable reluctance and a degree of discomfort with the video process, but the benefits that came with the dialogue, support – the inspiration often found – soon far outweighed this for most. Staff identified for themselves, with the support of the Teaching and Learning Team, areas they wanted to look deeper into and work on and things they wanted to improve, and they were very keen to meet again for further discussion.

The Magenta Principles

Mike then introduced us to the Magenta Principles on a memorable day when we pretended to be a rock disintegrating in a desert! There is no doubt that we immediately grasped the significance of the ideas and bought into the philosophy of the Magenta Principles from the outset.

As a team, we first experimented with all that Mike had presented us with during our workshops; we filmed ourselves and sat together, reflecting on our own practice and developing a deeper understanding of the Magenta Principles approach. This allowed us to talk to colleagues with passion and understanding about strategies and concepts that had been personally tried and tested.

We then led a workshop to introduce the rest of the staff to the Magenta Principles and encouraged them to incorporate just one principle into their teaching over the coming weeks. Next, we led further workshops in which we went deeper with some of the principles, and supported staff in trying to incorporate new principles into their teaching. At first we just supported staff in *adopting* the use of the principles as an approach, but as confidence grew, we illustrated how the principles could be *adapted* and both encouraged and supported them in doing so.

Colleagues soon realised how easily the Magenta Principles could be adapted and implemented as a philosophy underpinning their teaching; the terminology of the principles almost became less important as they realised much of its benefit lay in the shared common language that facilitated discussion as opposed to assigning a label to an activity. Early on in our journey there were questions along the lines of but is it a sequence activity or an assemble activity? As confidence and understanding grew, teachers realised that the important thing was not what it was called but that the nature of the activity would improve our teaching and the children's learning – regardless of what term we assigned to it.

Teaching and Learning Team
Sidmouth CE Primary School

Teaching is exciting and innovative.

Whitley Bay High School
Ofsted 2013

Whitley Bay High School

As was suggested at the beginning of the book, Whitley Bay High School (WBHS) in the North East is the school that has taken the Magenta Principles to heart more than any other. In their own words:

"if our goal was to make learning an engaging, student-centred experience then the Magenta Principles was the vehicle that enabled us to get there."

There are some key words in that statement: *our, vehicle, us.* For WBHS did not simply adopt the Magenta Principles, they adapted them. More than that they developed and customised them and, over a number of years, arrived at a pedagogy that is distinctly theirs. They did it – the Magenta Principles were just a vehicle; a vehicle that helped them go on a most amazing journey.

The story of their journey is well worth telling, not so other schools can retrace their route but to simply provide one or two signposts that may prove useful to you on your travels.

Before the school tells its story, it is important to point out that – although those directly involved would be too modest to say it – Whitley Bay is an extraordinary school. In 2010 it was not only judged to be outstanding by Ofsted, it was awarded a grade one in all 31 categories with no issues for action. In 2013 it repeated the feat of being graded one in every category (by 2013 there were four categories).

However, what makes WBHS extraordinary is that this feat was achieved without sacrificing children, learning and enjoyment. Indeed, Ofsted described lessons as *exciting and innovative* – I would describe them as typically wow!

Whitley Bay – and there are other schools like it – destroy the myth that you can *either* have lessons that are fun and interesting *or* you have examination and Ofsted success. You can quite simply have both. Too often these days Ofsted wags the dog. Examination and inspection success is the unrelenting focus and pursued at the expense of learning. People tell me that lessons can't be fun and interesting in the current climate. Whitley Bay tells me otherwise.

Students and staff alike understand that the development of teaching is at the heart of the school. As such, there is a 'buzz' amongst adults and students in the classroom.

Whitley Bay High School
Ofsted 2013

The journey begins

It was an innocent question asked at an NQT induction session – *where exactly does learning happen in a lesson and how do you know?* – that prompted the leaders of teaching and learning at Whitley Bay High School to first approach Mike Hughes more than 10 years ago; we invited him into our school so that he could explore with us the kind of searching questions we found in his publications. The section of his book *Closing the Learning Gap*, which deals with what students are doing when learning is happening, chimed exactly with some classroom-based research we had carried out that suggested that good learning is invariably messy and rarely happens when the teacher is talking.

Mike's early whole staff training sessions at Whitley Bay had a significant impact because of the way he explored with us new notions of the teacher as a facilitator of learning. His visual representation of teacher talk (highlighted in red) in a lesson juxtaposed with student talk (highlighted in blue) helped us rewrite our lesson plans. This culminated in a moment of revelation: our most outstanding teachers were inclined to talk less, specifically in the opening ten minutes of the lesson, and question more. Moreover, significant chunks of their lessons were devoted to students working together or independently to make sense of the task for themselves with timely mini-plenaries helping them consolidate and reflect (see page 180).

> "Our challenge was to ensure all teachers moved their lessons from red to blue, and in Mike's Magenta Principles we found a simple and effective way of helping them do this."

It is interesting to reflect that none of this seems particularly radical now, but it certainly was when we first embarked on our shared learning journey back in 2001.

Mike's training is peppered with metaphor (the pun is deliberate!) and phrases like *Good teachers give the picture – great teachers let students join up the dots* (see page 149) have helped our staff conceptualise his approach. In recent years we have been experimenting with strategies that best facilitate the processing stage of knowledge acquisition; it's back to the original question in a way – *where exactly does learning happen in a lesson and how do you know?* – because we have become much more acutely aware of what students are doing to make meaning for themselves.

The leadership of the school has created an ethos where discussing and developing teaching is the norm. This contributes greatly to the quality of teaching at the school being outstanding.

Whitley Bay High School
Ofsted 2013

Teaching and learning is our priority

Teaching and learning has for many years been the first priority at WBHS. This is an easy and not a particularly dramatic claim to make. The key, however, is to back up the rhetoric with action.

We believe that teaching and learning cannot be divorced from:

- Leadership
- Professional development.

Therefore, if teaching and learning is the priority, there are clear implications for the style of school leadership. Similarly, we believe that a commitment to high quality teaching and learning requires a commitment to high quality professional development. Consequently…

- It was as far back as 2002 when our governors – on the recommendation of the senior team – took the very brave decision to send students home an hour early each Tuesday so that we could engage in a high quality training programme (more details page 207).
- In 2006 we introduced a Teaching and Learning Observation Gallery (more details page 209).
- The Headteacher attends every training session.

The last point is particularly important. If teaching and learning is our focus, then it has to be central to the daily work of each member of the leadership team. There is an expectation that responsibility post-holders will model outstanding teaching and training, and that they will prioritise their own teaching to credibly contribute to the debate about great learning.

CPD at WBHS

Our journey to outstanding has been genuinely exhilarating. When we launched our Tuesday afternoon CPD programme over 10 years ago we could not have predicted what a dramatic leap in achievement would follow, or how the Teaching and Learning Observation Gallery we introduced in 2006 would focus our attention so forensically on the craft of teaching.

On his first visit to the school, Mike Hughes had asked us *is there an explicit shared definition of learning in your school?* In response to our somewhat sketchy reply he had added, *because if you want something to happen you need to make it explicit – don't leave it to chance.* Tuesday training has become the route to crystallising our

...we do with teachers what we ask teachers to do with students.

definition of learning year after year as each new cohort of starter teachers move up through the profession with us to promotion elsewhere: but arguably more importantly, it has proved inclusive and affirming to experienced career teachers who value a regular opportunity to shape the debate and take it forward.

There are five key dimensions to our approach to CPD:

- Four weekly training cycle – CPD sessions explicitly model the style and structure of lessons we want teachers to adapt in the classroom
- No routine grading of lesson observations
- Teaching and Learning Observation Gallery
- Cross-curricular 'Tag' observations
- Induction.

Week 1 CPD

The highlight of our four weekly teaching and learning training programme is week 1. Our house style for whole staff training has gradually evolved into a model now recognized as *the Whitley Way*, which mirrors a typical lesson. Just like our students in the classroom, our teachers are seated for training in carefully differentiated cross-curricular groups using name cards (see page 77) to signal their place; activities are highly interactive, often playful in intent and structured to promote deep reflection. In other words, we do with teachers what we ask teachers to do with students.

In these sessions the emphasis is on new ideas, intellectual challenge, pace and engagement. We collaborate in a non-hierarchical way, blending youth and experience, realism and optimism, laughter and solemnity in equal measure. This shared endeavour promotes both self-esteem and well-being leading to high morale. The leadership team, including the Headteacher, makes training a number one priority and participates alongside their peers in all CPD activities.

Week 1 is usually led by one of our *teaching and learning groups,* who from as far back as 1998 have carried out classroom-based research on key priorities for improvement. Typically composed of five teachers at different stages of their career, these groups change each year and are led by one of our leadership team or our lead trainers. We deliberately include all heads of department or heads of year, who are new to the school in a group as soon as they arrive, so that they will get a weekly injection of ethos and CPD, and immediately become part of a group generating creative thinking about new ways to raise achievement. In turn, we get an insight into their very different experiences from other schools and their reflective thoughts on what they like and dislike about our strategies here.

Teachers are committed to improving their craft as professionals.

Whitley Bay High School
Ofsted 2013

No routine grading of lesson observations

We are one of those few brave schools nationally that have never routinely graded lessons and yet we achieved 31 outstanding grades in our Ofsted inspection of March 2010, when 90% of teaching was deemed good or outstanding. Our annual performance management cycle involves lesson observations, but there is no checklist or formula, no numbers, and no overreliance on the latest Ofsted framework. Crucially, our main interest is to observe the learners, and that way we can use the coaching model we developed with Mike to underpin our targets for each teacher. It is predicated on the principle that it is all right to have a poor lesson providing we can all learn from it.

Observation Gallery

Investing in a Teaching and Learning Observation Gallery in 2006 acted as a huge catalyst for teachers to improve their practice by observing their peers. The gallery allows teachers to observe covertly accompanied by a coach who facilitates a debate throughout the lesson; but crucially no judgements or grades are ever recorded as part of this process. Our interest is not in perfect lessons that go uniquely well but in the small details that demonstrate the teacher's mastery of their craft – such as how to integrate a latecomer successfully into a task or how to come up with a spontaneous Magenta Principle to 'capture' a learning moment not anticipated in the original lesson plan. Testament to the success of our approach came from Ofsted in 2010, who commented that our less successful teachers were attempting to emulate the characteristics of our best – they knew what great learning looked like but they were less skilful at bringing it about.

Tag observations

The PE department at WBHS inspired the idea of *Tag* lesson observations. When playing *tag*, one person touches the next who becomes *it*, until they tag someone else in turn. We use *Tag* observations – teacher A observes teacher B who in turn observes teacher C – in order to follow a trail or to carry out research; for example, we have analysed aspects of classroom practice such as the quality and frequency of praise in lessons or the use of short focused writing tasks via Tag observations.

Induction

Since 2008 we have devised an NQT and new staff induction morning, which revolves around the fundamental question: *What do children do to make sense of information?* The first session based around a fairytale theme accessible to all is entitled *Pace and Challenge*, and it serves to introduce all new staff to seven of the Magenta Principles: change, reduce, assemble, prioritise, sequence, arrange and connect. By having a narrative thread as you would in a lesson, with an engaging theme, we use the principles to illustrate how learning can be sequenced to add pace and coherence, stretch and challenge.

In a nutshell, our philosophy is this: excite and engage your teachers and they will enthuse and motivate your learners in their turn.

Whitley Baying

Mike consistently makes the point in his training that you can't simply adopt things. It is a philosophy we share and nothing we do is off the peg. The school ethos is one of developing teaching and learning by finding the answer in the room; a large teaching staff has an infinitely wide range of skills and interests to share and the role of senior leadership is to structure planning and training so that as many individuals as possible can impact positively on the work of their peers.

While we are confident in our own internal expertise and develop a great many things in-house, we would also acknowledge a range of external influences on our practice over the last decade or more. In addition to Mike, the work of Daniel Goleman, Alistair Smith, Guy Claxton and Spencer Kagan has played a significant part and helped shape and guide our thinking on teaching and learning.

Crucially, we did not adopt a single externally developed model, framework or approach in its entirety. Rather, we have been selective; taking what we considered to be the best and relevant bits from a variety of educationalists, customising them and ending up with an approach that is distinctly Whitley Bay in flavour.

Everyone a learner

The school's core values are at the heart of all developments and decision making. Based on a culture of emotional intelligence, boundless optimism, commitment, energy, hard work and, most importantly, fun, we want all staff and students to conspicuously enjoy coming to school. Everyone from the Headteacher to the youngest student is invited to consider themselves primarily as a learner and to understand how significantly they can contribute to the school's development.

Moreover the school's organisation revolves around making opportunities for teachers to work together creatively to make every hour of every day have the maximum benefit for both learner and teacher. It wouldn't be an understatement to say that research excites us because innovation is something to be welcomed; a high percentage of our staff is involved in the dissemination of groundbreaking practice generated here and from other schools across the region, the country and the world. In a nutshell, our philosophy is this: excite and engage your teachers and they will enthuse and motivate your learners in their turn, and this has emerged primarily from our work with Mike Hughes.

This school is not complacent. The school fully understands that 'outstanding does not mean perfect' and there are comprehensive development plans in place to improve teaching even further.

Whitley Bay High School
Ofsted 2010

Reflections from the outside

As an outsider – albeit an outsider who has worked closely with the school over many years – a number of things strike me about the way teaching and learning has developed at WBHS:

- The process of internalising – or *Whitley Baying* – is crucial. Staff at the school understand and commit to the approach, not least because they have been fully involved in developing it. Consequently, teachers are not using Magenta Principle activities because they are expected to or for the sake of it, but because of a deeply held belief that they promote exciting and effective learning.

- WBHS walk the talk. Everyone claims teaching and learning is the priority, but few schools follow things through to their logical conclusion.

- This manifests itself in their professional development programme, which is exceptional. It is no coincidence that the schools with the best teaching and learning also have the best CPD programmes.

- The conscious commitment to enthusing teachers so they may in turn enthuse learners is as significant as it is unusual these days. How many schools make explicit reference to having fun? How many schools strive to ensure that *all staff and students enjoy coming to school and love the process of learning?*

- The aim was NOT to achieve an Ofsted outstanding. The aim was to enthuse and motivate in order to promote exciting and effective learning. Ofsted success was an outcome not a goal.

- The school does not stand still. The prevailing culture of research and development ensures that teachers are constantly reflecting upon and developing practice still further. Indeed, Ofsted make explicit reference to the fact that the school is not complacent and is always looking to improve.

It would be appropriate to leave the last word to Adam Chedburn, who was Headteacher of the school between 1993 and 2014. In the foreword he refers to the moment in *Alice in Wonderland* when Alice meets the Cheshire Cat at a crossroads. The Cat suggests to Alice that the direction she should take is dependent upon where she wants to get to. Whitely Bay High School knew exactly where it wanted to get to.

My understanding of the Magenta Principles has meant a 180 degree shift in the planning of my lessons. I now plan lessons for learning rather than teaching, and the Magenta Principles are key in that. They are not a set of activities or a resource; I prefer to see them as a sort of camera filter, like using Instagram, where you can apply it to any existing technique/resource/activity, which changes the experience of that technique/resource/activity.

To view them this way meant I didn't have to change completely the way I teach. I didn't have to start from scratch in my effort to challenge my students more. I could use all of the activities I'd built up in the decade of experience I'd already gained, but I could tweak them all to make them much more focused on pupil learning.

Justine Connolly
Carlton le Willows Academy, Nottingham

Finally...

There is only one possible way to close this book – with a Magenta Principle.

Which, for you, has been the most significant:

- *page in the book?*
- *word in the book?*
- *theme of the book?*

There are many contenders for the most significant page in the book: page 21 when the connection was made between the maths lesson *(do the three hardest)* and the English lesson *(who was the key character?)*; page 33 and the suggestion that we need to think *principles not strategies* or page 147 when it was empasised that the Magenta Principles are not ready meals but dependent upon the teacher to facilitate the learning experience.

While all of the above undoubtedly have a claim, I would suggest that the most significant page was 27 and the idea that **a minor change in practice can lead to a significant shift in emphasis.** This point was illustrated by highlighting the difference between *read page 7* and *have a look at page 7 and tell me which you think is the most important sentence.* It is such a simple strategy yet the moment we ask them to do something with page 7 – reduce it – rather than just read it, we begin to switch the emphasis from passive to active, occupied to engaged, knowing to understanding. It is a page that is well worth another read.

I would go on to suggest that the choice of the most important word is rather more clear-cut and that, by some considerable distance, the most significant word in the book is *and*. For by making these relatively minor changes to practice we can both tick the boxes, cover the curriculum, help children pass exams, achieve inspection success **and** have engaging, exciting learning taking place in our classrooms.

And the most important theme? The answer to that can be found on page 15.

This was always intended to be a book with a difference; not so much a book for you to read, more a book for you to write.

Now is the time for you to pick up your pen.

Answers

Page 56 Grandmother's Song

Correct order of images: *B A C*

Correct final sentence: *B – No matter where we are grandmother is never far away. And whenever we need her we can simply shut our eyes and feel her hold us so very close.*

Page 94

B=1
A=2
D=4
G=9
E=13
R=15

When placed in numerical order…BADGER!

Page 132 Icelandic lyrics

Teachers who have contributed to this book

Michael Kelly, Rachel Hayward, Anthony Smith, Mike Hughes, Gemma Gilbert, Ellie Hughes, Holly Burrow, Paul Rogers, Rache Stone, Rebecca Cooper, Nikki Ashton, Louise King, Sam Evans

Whitley Bay High School
Rachel Mays, Linda Buckle, Chris Johnson, Andrew Burton, Hilary Ratcliffe, Simon Mooney, Paul Rochester, David Lee, Louise Bradley, Adam Rule, Fiona Hepton, Janice Burrow, Adam Chedburn, Alan Keegan, Simon Hall, Phil Bell, Katie Fokias, Andy Cole, Kerry Lord, Steve Williams, Steve Wilson, Ellie Lee (student)

Sidmouth CE Primary School
Emma Johns, Joanna Rousseau, Rachel Earley, Gareth Bemister, Josh Bashford, Cheryl Paterson, Meryl Logan, Leah Stratton, Paul Walker

Wymondham High Academy
Jackie Everett, Jonathan Rockey, Layla Hill, Lynn Stevenson, Lyn Ottaway, Emma Perchard

Pinders Primary School, Wakefield
Gina Bedford

Lutterworth College
Sara Raywood, Lauren Freemantle, Sukhi Sarai, Abigail Lear, Michelle Thresher, Emily Perkins

The Ecclesbourne School
Tom Walton, Sara DelGaudio, Emma Clark, Lisa Walton

Shenley Brook End School, Milton Keynes
Chris Holmwood, Nigel Cross

Trinity School, Carlisle
Suzanne McArdle, Emma Joyce, Andrew Palmer, Jo Hawkin, Declan McArdle, Linda Hodgson

Ysgol Bro Dinefwr, Llandeilo
Rachel Nicholson

Carlton le Willows Academy, Nottingham
Justine Connolly, Jamie Boyer, Pascal Broadley

St Augustine's RC High School, Billington, Lancashire
Rebecca Burton, Bev Bury, Nathan Moorby, Emma Smith, Kay Jameson, Caroline Pope, Catherine Gunn, Joanna Rutter, Helen Holt.

Ysgol Gyfun Gymraeg Bro Myrddin, Croesyceiliog
Ben Williamson

St Thomas More Catholic School, Blaydon-upon-Tyne
Luke McEnaney, Katie Spurr, Christine Brown

Yenton Primary School, Erdington, Birmingham
Liz Webster

The Brunts Academy, Mansfield
Hally Lockwood

All Saints Catholic School, Dagenham
Tony Purkiss

Chiltern Training Group
Sarah Doe, Lara Morse, Dean Sandford, Anna-Lisa Doering

Brinsworth Comprehensive School, Rotherham
Jenny Kemp, John Naylor, Elizabeth Montgomery

Richard Bonington Primary and Nursery School, Nottingham
Nick Smith

Acknowledgements

The following individuals and organisations have kindly given permission to reproduce their work.

Page 48: *L'oiseau lune jaune* by Joan Miró reproduced with kind permission of Fundació Joan Miró, Barcelona © Successio Miro / ADAGP Paris and DACS London 2014

L'oiseau lune jaune
1963
Etching and aquatint
Edition : 75 copies (56,5 x 79 cm) on Rives (75 x 104,5 cm),
numbered and signed, and some not for sale signed copies.
Publisher: Maeght éditeur
Printer: Maeght, Levallois-Perret
Photographer: Jaume Blassi

Page 56: Text and images from *Grandmother's Song* by Barbara Soros Illustrated by Jackie Morris, reproduced with kind permission of the publishers – Barefoot Books Limited, Bristol

Page 90: Image: 7959 Artist(s): LS Lowry Title: Punch & Judy (3), 1947 Medium: Reproductive lithograph Dimensions: 49.5 x 76 cm Credit: © The Estate of LS Lowry. All Rights Reserved, DACS 2014. Image: © Arts Council Collection, Southbank Centre

Page 108 : Extract from *Havisham* by Carol Ann Duffy. Copyright © Carol Ann Duffy 2103. Reproduced by permission of the author c/o Rogers, Coleridge & White Ltd., 20 Powis Mews, London W11 1JN

Page 117: *The Tapestry of Truths and Beliefs* by Grayson Perry. © Getty Images News / Photographer: Peter Macdiarmid

Page 117: *Hereford Mappa Mundi of 1280* showing Jerusalem at the centre Europe is lower left Africa is lower right. © North Wind Pictures / Alamy

Page 120: Extract from *A River, of Course* from *Poems for the Geography Classroom* by Mark Cowan, reproduced with kind permission of the publishers – Educational Printing Services Limited, Blackburn 2008

Page 129: *Supper at Emmaus* by Caravaggio, 1601 © FineArt/Alamy

Images on pages 76, 125, 127 (motorbike and lake), 136, 138 sourced by 123RF
Image on page 127 (train) sourced by iStock

Other books referred to in this publication

The Black Book of Colours by Menena Cottin and Rosana Faria
(Walker Books Limited, London 2010)

Smart Schools by David Perkins
(The Free Press 1992)

Grandmother's Song by Barbara Soros Illustrated by Jackie Morris
(Barefoot Books Limited, Bristol 1998)

Poems for the Geography Classroom by Mark Cowan
(Educational Printing Services Limited, Blackburn 2008)

Mean Time by Carol Ann Duffy
(Picador 2013)

Lessons are for Learning by Mike Hughes
(Bloomsbury Publishing 1997)

Closing the Learning Gap by Mike Hughes
(Bloomsbury Publishing 1999)

Strategies for Closing the Learning Gap by Mike Hughes
(Bloomsbury Publishing 2001)

Tweak to Transform by Mike Hughes
(Bloomsbury Publishing 2002)

And the Main Thing is…Learning

By Mike Hughes

In short, this book is about how to make learning the main thing – for pupils and teachers – and argues that the future, in terms of both pedagogy and policy, demands an approach rooted in learning.

More specifically, it suggests that:

- everything we do must be based explicitly upon learning
- teachers must be learners too
- we have a professional responsibility to go on learning about learning, because the better we understand learning and the learning process the better able we are to facilitate it in others.

The key question, and the one that this book seeks to address, is whether the strategies and policies that have enabled us to improve teaching and raise standards will be sufficient to help us develop further and promote learning. Is it more of the same, or do we need a change of emphasis if we are break through the inevitable plateau of attainment and achievement?

'This book is of great importance to the nation. It provides a compass direction, a route map and a set of tactics that will enable us to achieve the educational goals that matter most.

And the Main Thing is…Learning does not lambast; it does not criticise or destroy; rather it questions, challenges and connects. It looks back and looks forward, consolidating the territory we have gained and providing further bridges for us to cross as we continue the journey from where we are to where we need to go.'

Paul Ginnis, *author of The Teacher's Toolkit*

For more details and to order a copy of *And the Main Thing is…Learning* please visit: **www.mikehughes-ets.co.uk**

Mike Hughes:
Education Training and Support

Mike Hughes is a highly acclaimed trainer and author of a number of hugely influential books including *And the Main thing is…Learning, Closing the Learning Gap* and *Tweak to Transform*. After spending 18 years as a teacher, most recently as a secondary head, he now works full time supporting schools and organisations in the drive to improve learning in the classroom.

Mike's work is hugely varied and tailored to fit the needs of the individual school / teacher. Anyone considering working with Mike is invited to contact him to discuss their requirements and explore possibilities.

To give you a flavour of his work…

Focus
He works predominately in three inter-related areas

- Teaching and learning
- Coaching
- Leadership development and leadership for learning

Group size
- Anything from 1 to 500+
- senior leadership teams
- clusters and networks
- teaching and learning coaches
- Headteacher organisations
- working groups
- middle leaders
- individual teachers
- NQT conferences

Organisation
The possibilities are endless:

- keynote address
- staff training day
- twilight inset
- a programme of on-going support

Some schools invite Mike to run an inset day while others have worked with him for a number of years.

Contact details: **T: 07833030987 E: mikehughes.ets@gmail.com
W: www.mikehughes-ets.co.uk**

The Magenta Principles Workshops

Focusing upon engagement, depth and challenge in the classroom

Mike is running a series of one day workshops to accompany the launch of his new book, *The Magenta Principles*. All delegates will receive a free copy of the book.

The main areas of focus:

- Practical strategies that both excite and engage

- Teaching for understanding

- Getting the balance between achieving examination and Ofsted success AND teaching lessons that are interesting and enjoyable

- Switching the emphasis from occupied to engaged, knowing to understanding, teaching to learning

- Using the Magenta Principles to improve questioning

- Implications for Professional Development.

The day will be workshop style with a series of practical, hands-on sessions and is designed to introduce delegates to a range of Magenta Principle activities and further develop the ideas found in this book.

Due to the workshop nature of the event **places are strictly limited.**

The day is suitable for classroom teachers (KS2 – KS5) and school leaders who have responsibility for leading Teaching and Learning.

Full details of Magenta Principles Workshops, including dates, venues and how to book can be found at **www.mikehughes-ets.co.uk**

Mike Hughes **T: 07833030987 E: mikehughes.ets@gmail.com**